Winning at Life

Realizing True Success in Business and in Life

(Principles of Winning at Life That Change Lives Forever)

Quinton Predovic

Published By **Elena Holly**

Quinton Predovic

Winning at Life: Realizing True Success in Business and in Life (Principles of Winning at Life That Change Lives Forever)

ISBN 978-1-77485-901-8

Legal & Disclaimer

The information contained in this ebook is not designed to replace or take the place of any form of medicine or professional medical advice. The information in this ebook has been provided for educational & entertainment purposes only.

The information contained in this book has been compiled from sources deemed reliable, and it is accurate to the best of the Author's knowledge; however, the Author cannot guarantee its accuracy and validity and cannot be held liable for any errors or omissions. Changes are periodically made to this book. You must consult your doctor or get professional medical advice before using any of the suggested remedies, techniques, or information in this book.

Table Of Contents

Chapter 1: Create Awesome Habits

Consistency

"Successful people are simply those with successful habits."

– Brian Tracy

According to the Merriam Webster dictionary, to be consistent means marked in harmony, regularity, and steady continuity. To show consistency in any form and any area of our lives means that you are in harmony with the task, and it comes with a sense of association and belief.

In your daily routines, there are things that you practice daily. You have formed a habit here. The small tasks that you have mastered on the cellular level, you perform without thinking, and efficiently. Think about brushing your teeth, taking a shower, and your daily upkeep. You can see that this task, practiced once, does not pay, but repetitive practice and consistency brings you the result. I believe that you were somewhat positively reinforced at the beginning, which made you repeat them over and over again, craving for the same results. To win in your life and business, in the belief of the result you are aiming at, practice the daily task; you will be rewarded, which causes you to repeat—we create our lives by the habits that we consistently practice. If you have always eaten right, it pays off someday, perhaps with vibrancy at old age. If you have healthy teeth, I bet you continuously visited your dentist and practiced consistent hygiene.

In business, have you wondered about consistent reward with your pay? If you do not put in the daily consistent business practices that yield reward, it sure will show in your bank account. It will affect promotions and business growth. When I did network marketing, we were coached to make a least six calls a day and to get fresh leads. With that many calls, which wasn't easy for me, I hardly closed any sales, at least not initially. But when I looked at the numbers, making six calls a day, and following up on some old leads, done consistently, yielded sales. You see, that took consistent action, which was a habit. I read that professional basketball players take countless shots on and off the basketball court. The constant activities show up in the games. This goes for any sport-building muscle memory with consistent and ethical practices. No wonder professionals practice the same routine, pre-game, at warm-ups, and post-game.

I am telling you to practice consistency in your daily lives and business. If something shows to work at first or has been proven, raise your game by exercising it, and consistently. It will pay off, and you will be an all-around winner.

"In essence, if we want to direct our lives, we must take control of our consistent actions. It's not what we do once in a while that shapes our lives, but what we do consistently."

– Tony Robbins

Designing Your Life by Choice

"Be miserable. Or motivate yourself. Whatever has to be done, it's always your choice."

– Wayne Dyer

The power of choice is a privilege that comes with being human, and especially at this time, where life is much more comfortable and with many accessories to make it more manageable. It is a beautiful world because you have the choice to design it exactly how you want it. The power of choice will give you options, and you can take care in selecting what it is that you want.

I interviewed a few friends and acquaintances on the process they use in making choices. Yours will be similar. Some decisions come easy, like what to wear on a cold winter day—yes, I bet you chose right by choosing warm clothing. Some other choices are not so easy, like what business to do, and business partner. Please choose wisely, as good choices every time makes it easier when the challenging time arises. For example, by choosing to build better relationships and community, networking with the right people, you then will attract superstars to your business and your life. By making good daily choices with your finances, you can afford the vacation or retirement of your dream. By choosing to wake up every morning to exercise instead of sleeping in, you will be investing in good health.

I want you to create good habits when it comes to making choices about your life and business. I encourage you to choose in alignment with your values. The reason why your company has a mission statement is so that you have a guide, and so should your life. If your mission statement is well stated and defined, making everyday choices should be more comfortable and empowering.

Know that every choice you make affects your life. So with every opportunity, choose to create the experience, the one you will be glad to meet now and in the future. In a case where you make a wrong choice, let it go, take it as a learning experience, and choose wisely next time.

Winning is a day-to-day endeavor. I am choosing to finish this chapter even though it is a day after Christmas, and I could be with friends and family. I want to schedule my time well, and allow critical activities so that I can complete my book in a month. I want you to pay attention and take inventory of all the decisions and choices you make in a day. In 24 hours, how easy was it? Was it in alignment with your values? Did you check in with your mission statement? Repeat the next day. The goal of this exercise is to make you understand the frequency and the amount of opportunity you have daily to create your life. Choose to be a winner!

"From now on, it is only through a conscious choice, and through a deliberate policy that humanity can survive."

– Pope John Paul II

In Flow or in the Zone

"Water is the softest of all things, yet it is the most powerful. The ocean patiently allows all things to flow into it. It is always flexible. The Tao is not about grasping, but allowing, like water."

– Wayne Dyer

To be in Flow, or in the zone, means to proceed smoothly and steadily. A term familiar to many creatives and athletes, in this state, they can create their best work and with depth. Perhaps you have experienced moments in your life and business where time passed by, and you paid no attention to time. I think this must be the moment when you are in harmony with your work. In peak performance, the artists become superhuman. Think of Mozart or Bach, co-creating with the universe. I encourage you to love what you do, working with a skill with so much passion that it requires the universe to join in. I doubt that the world will want to co-create mediocre work—no, I do not think so! You must cherish your life and business to give it the attention, and focus on something for a while. Winning requires that you are doing work that is important to you; it must be work that takes some skill and is somewhat challenging. When you conquer this task, driving through it in Flow and in the zone, then that is winning. It will be different for everyone, but please choose your work meaningfully.

I have found that early in the morning is the time I typically will get in Flow. I can hear myself better and can get into my work. At this time, everything is magical. I can exert less energy, be in full focus, and work for a more extended period.

For you to be successful in your life and at work, you must develop success habits— habits that create and not destroy; practices that sustain and not evade. Please make it your duty to be diligent in choosing work that helps you tap into your creative side by being present and in Flow.

Creating with your supernatural power makes you a winner. You probably have work you started and never finished. Maybe you started to write a book but gave up after a few chapters. The reason why you quit was that you did not give it enough attention, intensity, focus, and emotions required to get in the zone. For any significant work or project to come to completion, you must experience Flow, and you should recognize it each time and become good friends with it. I urge you to get that project, dust it off, and start again, but this time do it differently to get into peak performance and bring the work to completion.

"When I am traveling in a carriage or walking after a good meal, or during the night when I cannot sleep, it is on such occasions that ideas flow best and most abundantly."

– Wolfgang Amadeus Mozart

Discipline

"To enjoy good health, to bring true happiness to one's family, to bring peace to all, one must first discipline and control one's mind. If a man can control his mind, he can find the way to Enlightenment, and all wisdom and virtue will naturally come to him."

– Buddha

My best definition of discipline is the training expected to produce a specific character or pattern of behavior, especially training that produces moral or mental improvement. I cannot think of anything I have done worthwhile that did not require discipline on my part. The restraint exercised over my impulses, emotions, and desires is an order and pattern of behavior that will determine a moral character.

You may have dreams. The desire to reach your goals may be there, but without discipline, you will be unable to take the prescribed steps to complete the activities required to make your dream come true. The training to show up every day and perform at your best and consistently requires discipline to act against emotions. That in itself is self-control.

The habits you have, and the order you have in your life and business, describe your results. Look through your daily routine and ritual—are there activities that require a high level of structure, almost with the instructions set by self and not by others? Think about the New Year resolutions; the small percentage of people that stay on track for 30 days can maintain it because they have discipline. It is the reason why most New Year resolutions are broken in about a week— lacking the order and structure to support activities will lead to many disappointments.

Many lifestyle habits will generally require a set order. If you have fitness or wellness goals, there will be emotions and opposing behaviors that will distract you. Still, the ability to stick with the recommended instructions will yield results, since these rituals are to be exercised for an extended period to get the result. The discipline is crucial, or you will fall off the wagon in no time.

It will take discipline to play at the level required to win in your personal life and business. Whatever that means to you, any act done at this high level is not natural and usually not very pleasant, but repetition is what says you are a trained winner. Athletes are very familiar with this term, and that is why, with the ups and downs, they repeat the daily work. The discipline to write every day for at least 20 minutes will complete my book in no time.

When you are a person of discipline, you are a person of high quality. People will notice you because you will consistently show up in your life and business; it shows in your performances, and you will become a top producer and will have structure and order in your life and industry.

"Read some good, heavy, serious books just for discipline: Take yourself in hand and master yourself."

– W.E.B. Du Bois

 Dedication

"The best way to find yourself is to lose yourself in the service of others."

– Mahatma Gandhi

Without self-sacrifice, nothing significant is realized. Hard work and dedication usually come together. When you have belief in a cause, project, or mission, you have to stay dedicated to do whatever necessary to be successful. That typically will come through hard work and a lot of sacrifices. If you are dedicated to a specific aspect of your business, you definitely will follow through on the tasks required to make things happen. It might require working longer hours, seeking new partnerships, or even making some new enemies. For example, if you are dedicated to customer service, satisfaction, and getting training, the way you run your business will certainly reflect your mission.

In Arizona, in the summertime, the temperature can be over 110 degrees. It is not uncommon to see athletes train in such brutal weather. If you believe in the cause—maybe it is winning the championship—you will sacrifice the discomfort to get the results and successes that you want.

If something is important to you, a little bit of dedication—focus, time, energy—will bring that to light. Your life purpose requires you to be intentional and diligent to live up to your full potential. Things don't just happen. They happen because you take time to nurture the purpose. Have you ever seen a business with a dedicated staff, even specialized front desk staff, sold on the business mission? The company will thrive because the team will nourish it with enthusiasm and creativity, because they believe in the cause or the business. Anything that you do without dedication is not capable of reaching the highest potential.

Decide what is most important to you in your life and business, and give maximum attention and priority—spreading yourself too thin does not help. Hence, Jack of all trades, master of none. Who are you? What is your brand, and who does your business represent? These are some of the questions that can get you started in concluding. Before you commit to anything, ask yourself, why do I want this? If your "why" isn't big enough, then you may not have the resiliency to follow through with the day-to-day grind that will come with it. Staying busy is not the same as being productive. Since we have so much time in a day, choose what is most important to you; hopefully, it is tied with your mission. Stay dedicated, and win!

"There is always the danger that we may just do the work for the sake of the work. This is where the respect and the love and the devotion come in, that we do it to God, to Christ, and that's why we try to do it as beautifully as possible."

– Mother Teresa

Leadership

"Leadership is influence."

– John C. Maxwell

Leadership is an exciting topic. To be a leader in recent times has taken a different perspective, one with better understanding as the old definition and role of a leader has evolved.

The most popular definition of leadership, according to the Merriam Webster dictionary, is the capacity to guide the actions of a person or group. Synonyms include governance, management, control, direction, charge, and a host of other familiar terms. I want you to pause and answer the question, what does leadership mean to you? What quality should you look for in a leader?

I have found that the people I see and admire as leaders, generally have structure, are reliable, operate with integrity, and are empathic. For the most part, this is the primary qualities that influence me, and then I can be open to listen and follow.

In your life and business, I want you to be conversant about how your life and actions will affect the people close to you. As a leader, you want the best for people that follow, so your ultimate goal is to be a good example. I am not saying you should change in your personality and assume a position of inauthenticity. Be who you are when no one is watching. Authenticity is admirable. Bring the best of you to your people, work on honing your skills as a leader, and you will be unstoppable. Mastery of self yields confidence—since people you are leading want the assurance that you can guide them to a destination, you will have loyal followers.

It would be best if you had unique leadership attributes to lead in the families, communities, spiritual organizations, and corporations. But the fundamental key that will give you the authority is that you realize you are capable of making a difference. I believe God, nature, or the universe understands this better; hence, a child is born to a family. The mother and/or father are the first leaders. If you are a mother or father, you will instinctively take up the role of a leader, nurturing and guiding your young. I believe, as a parent, you are uniquely given the qualities and permission to lead by nature. The same authority or permit is also given to you around the different settings in your life and business. All you need to do is step into it with power and say yes! If you continuously say yes, in your life and business, seeing each opportunity as a chance to guide, direct, and manage, imagine the impact you will have in the world. You are a winner!

"Enlightened leadership is spiritual if we understand spirituality not as some religious dogma or ideology, but as the domain of awareness where we experience values like truth, goodness, beauty, love, and compassion, and also intuition, creativity, insight, and focused attention."

– Deepak Chopra

MAIN TAKEAWAYS

Chapter 2: Your Mindset

Living Your Purpose

"When I chased after money, I never had enough. When I got my life on purpose, and focused on giving of myself and everything that arrived into my life, then I was prosperous."

— Wayne Dyer

Your purpose is the reason why you are here on earth. I call it an assignment that you are bound to fulfill to live a happy life. It benefits others directly and in a specific way. It comes from you and from who you are, and it isn't surprising to find that most times, it is in simple activities. It will make you joyful. If you did a survey, that's how many people will describe you. Friends and family will describe you alike. It looks like a label. When you hear that people make an impact in the world, it is because they are living out their purpose; they are wired and equipped to make a difference in the lives of others in a specific way.

I was once only living, but started being when I recognized and acknowledged my purpose. Now when I act, I act with more intensity towards things that matter to me, and others that will help me live out my purpose. When I serve accordingly, it does not feel like work; there is much energy, passion, and creativity because it lights up my spirit. You must discover your purpose, and know it to the depth of your soul, so that when asked, you can speak it with power, and own it. You do not want to be a dabbler in life. I believe you will save a lot of time and energy, and even less agony and frustration, by targeting all your acts towards your purpose.

In your personal and professional life, it is imperative to build an environment that will make you successful in living a meaningful life according to your vision. It will help you make important decisions like where to live, your choice of partners, and the work environment. You will surely live a life of integrity. You will have faith in your journey if you do encounter difficulty; you are not discouraged, since you have confidence in your journey. It is essential for you. Beauty comes with living a life that adds value to you and others—a life of passion and a life of purpose.

It is essential that you win at the right things and that have meaning. I encourage you to map out your purpose and write it on paper so that it is clear; it certainly requires soul searching and meditating. When you can verbalize your objective, only then will you start living and winning.

"People who use time wisely, spend it on activities that advance their overall purpose in life."

– John C. Maxwell

On a Mission Every Day!

"Most employees only want to know how much they get paid and how much time off they get—they probably don't have the mission in their souls."

– Robert Kiyosaki

I realize that as you go about your day on a mission, you have enthusiasm and energy. The focus energizes you and puts fire in your belly. Hence, the difference from jumping out of bed vs. crawling out of bed. You will jump out of bed simply because you want to take on your day, with assignments and results to produce. Your mission will motivate you to set goals for each day, and you are focused on hitting the target. If you are on a mission, you are determined and unstoppable; there is no limit to the amount of work and type of work you are willing to undertake. You will become flexible since, honestly, there is no one way of getting to your target. It will make you get creative so that your customer is satisfied. I have had some days where I had no food or even water for an extended period because I was hyper focused to hit a target, and for a reason. Your mission causes you to make the impossible possible.

Having a mission for your life and business is a must. With a life mission, you are setting the benchmarks and the standards that you want to create as you pass through your life. Your task could also be dated: yearly, weekly, or even daily, but for the most part, the goals you set for your life and business are because of the mission that you want to achieve. The task you have, gives you force, tension, and urgency so that you are doing things with predictable outcomes and timelines. You probably crafted your mission, so it is a thing of pride. It is what you want to be known for—the image you want to present in your life and business. It is a personal standard from which you operate.

When you have a mission, you have structure and boundaries in your life and business. People around you will know your expectations, things you are willing to give, and what you are not ready to provide. And they will reciprocate. It is a beautiful thing when you can create boundaries because people appreciate why you act the way you do. I encourage you always to communicate your mission to the people involved in your life and business. They will take you seriously, and their expectations of how things ought to be around you will match. Think about what you stand for and what your business stands for, and establish a mission statement so that you are on target. That is winning!

"Everyone has his specific vocation or mission in life; everyone must carry out a concrete assignment that demands fulfillment. Therein he cannot be replaced, nor can his life be repeated; thus, everyone's task is unique as his specific opportunity to implement it."

– Viktor E. Frankl

Your Values

"I have learned that as long as I hold fast to my beliefs and values, and follow my own moral compass, then the only expectations I need to live up to are my own."

– Michelle Obama

One thing that I know is that you require rules to make anything worthwhile. Rules add structure to your life. You will be motivated to check your behaviors since they will come with consequences. Rules are enforced in the world in different places to impose order and discipline. It is even more appealing when you have your own personal laws that guide your actions and decisions.

Your values are the ideals that will guide your personal conduct. They are what will make you disagree on another person's actions. Typically, people will act from what they know, their experience, their belief, and all this will determine the set of rules and values that guide them. See, it is okay not to understand them, since you will be wearing different hats from the people you meet. You can even suggest that it will be easier to connect and partner with people of similar values. But you win when you acknowledge and respect other people's beliefs, but yet manage to adapt and keep in your power.

My values have helped me to act in ways that are congruent with who I am. There have been many situations where I made difficult decisions that were based on my values. I have also learned to question my values when needed, and the reason that I have chosen to go by any particular type of belief system. Becoming aware gives me the freedom to change.

The main advantage of having a value-based system is that it gives you standards. When you act by following your rules, you are being true to yourself; you are happier and more fulfilled. You will be guided to the right works and careers, and even to life partners that are of similar values. To have an increased sense of self is required to maintain the integrity and command of your life. With too many distractions nowadays, personal rules help you choose wisely. You can communicate what is relevant and meaningful to you, and you will also attract people with the same values, since they are looking for what you have or the culture.

I encourage you to be clear about your values, and to choose to apply them in your personal and professional life.

"Our words are always a reflection of the internal dialogue in our heads."

– Aya Fubara Eneli

Living Outside Your Comfort Zone

"If you put yourself in a position where you have to stretch outside your comfort zone, then you are forced to expand your consciousness."

– Les Brown

Your comfort zone is the level at which you function with ease and familiarity. In your comfort zone, you are safe and comfortable and can operate at your baseline without stretching yourself. It is a bubble that you surround yourself with to keep you safe. Still, the one thing I have noticed in my life, and others that I am around, is that the moment you venture outside this bubble, then soon, your life will begin to evolve. Your comfort zone is never constant; as soon as you adventure out and conquer one, you will replace it immediately.

I am a physical therapist, and I work with individuals to regain their function. I see firsthand the clinical examples and lessons in operating outside the comfort zone. It is what separates the toddler that takes a first step, or a stroke patient that sits up for the first time. In my profession, it is my responsibility to encourage my patients to complete tasks, and safely. I have seen that patients who decide to venture out of their comfort zone, progress faster. What hinders progress sometimes can be fear, amongst other factors. I have noticed that once a patient picks up the courage to try a new task, they can repeat, and with more repetition comes mastery. This is the same in your everyday living. For example, you may hesitate to speak in front of an unfamiliar crowd because you have never done such. Once you do it, you see that it isn't that bad after all, and with repetition, you gain confidence until you build another bubble.

For continuous growth in your life and business, you need to step outside your comfort zone, try new things to test yourself, and explore new options that you never knew were out there. Then new opportunities will begin pouring in, since you have stretched out. You will definitely give yourself the chance to perform at your peak, and that in itself will build confidence. Operating outside your comfort zone will help boost creativity and excitement, and will decrease burnout or boredom.

I encourage you to get uncomfortable with being safe and comfortable. Explore new adventure, expose yourself in different settings, build a relationship that is out of reach, and you will see that your business and life will expand. You can even implement a system to measure how many new things you try, bearing in mind to take on calculated risk, and always holding yourself responsible for creating unique experiences.

"Move out of your comfort zone. You can only grow if you are willing to feel awkward and uncomfortable when you try something new."

– Brian Tracy

Confidence Comes From Trying

"If you have no confidence in yourself, you are twice defeated in the race of life."

– Marcus Garvey

The dictionary meaning of confidence is a feeling or consciousness of one's powers or reliance on one's circumstance. In other words, faith in self, and a state of certainty. It is necessary to get your feet wet and see what is available to you in the first place. To think is not enough, but actively doing the task will make you build confidence. Action is required to win in any arena. You cannot win by thinking, wanting, or wishing. The moment you choose to undertake a task, there should be an initial period of awkwardness and difficulty, which is normal. This will apply to anything worthwhile that produces results, especially in high-level activities that would provide immense rewards and benefits. The awkwardness that you might experience initially is the beginning of amazing things that the future has in store for you. Confidence is the enabler that says, "Hey, you've been here before, and you can do it!" With each repetition, you are more and more convinced. You might even develop some tricks of your own. You will adapt, accommodate, whatever, but eventually, you will realize you have certainty and belief in yourself that you will act in the right order. The trust that you will continue to develop in yourself with each repeated act will eventually create more self-assurance and self-trust. But the truth is that all this wouldn't have occurred if you didn't get your feet wet in the first place.

I believe nothing is that difficult, especially when you have not tried. I have had some occasions where I was brave, took the first step in spite of fear and self-doubt, but found out that the activity wasn't that hard. The truth is that the movement might have been challenging. Still, by trying, I allowed myself to experience just a little success, which led to increased confidence.

You will need faith in yourself to succeed in anything. Confidence speaks louder than words. You will believe in your abilities, which gives you personal satisfaction. When you are confident, you accept who you are, and you give gratitude. You will freely give and receive compliments, and overall will be a positive person. You will influence people, and they will believe you, since you already believe in yourself. I encourage you never to limit yourself. Everything is possible if you care enough and think about it at all. Give it a try; you might never know. In science, the first action will form synapses and create new pathways in your brain, just from trying; and by repeating, you will refine and perfect. Love yourself enough to play full out in life; it is in working, in the little things, that you will experience victory.

"Inaction breeds doubt and fear. Action breeds confidence and courage. If you want to conquer fear, do not sit home and think about it. Go out and get busy."

– Dale Carnegie

Fun to Win

"I think we're having fun. I think our customers really like our products. And we're always trying to do better."

– Steve Jobs

Activities that are fun and bring you joy are worthwhile and engaging. And the excitement of winning is a pleasure to have. That is the reason why victory can become a habit, since you derive pleasure, making the behavior more than likely to repeat again and again to get the same results. Winning increases the dopamine level in the brain, which makes you feel better. You will feel great and pass it on to the people around you. When you are around winners or cheering for a winning team, you become joyful, because positivity is contagious. You do not want to undertake any challenge that will cause you to lose; usually, that is never anyone's intentions. Winning brings on instant reward; it is encouraging and will bring out the best in you. I have had some experiences where I was cheering for sports teams in sports arenas or even watching on television. I wasn't in a jersey, and it did not matter; I was joyful anyway when a group that I was cheering for won. I have no hesitation in bragging about "my team." We all want to associate with winners. Any events or competition that you undertake will allow you to apply yourself. The goal is to do well and have victory. Big wins or small wins, it does not matter; winning can be relative when you are having fun. We all need joy in our lives. It is essential to love what you do, and love it so much that you are having fun anyway. It helps increase your physical and psychological health and wellbeing, and will reduce stress and tolerance for pain. Have you watched a team performing and having fun? The relationships amongst team members are satisfying. This same principle can apply in your families and professional groups. When you are having fun, you are engaged, have no fear, and form close bonds. I encourage you to play to win in your life, but also to be strategic about planning to have fun. Create environments and events that make winning pleasurable. To prepare to be successful is winning already. Make efforts always to challenge yourself to create the joy and fulfillment you need to keep you focused—plan for pleasant experiences and enjoyments. Playfulness in your life is essential to add youthfulness and happiness. So when you are going through a challenge, stay focused, anticipate victory, but proactively set it up so that you can add some pleasure to your experience. It will help your overall attitude and wellbeing.

"It's kind of fun to do the impossible."

– Walt Disney

MAIN TAKEAWAYS

Chapter 3: Your Personal Growth And Development

Have a Plan for Your Personal Growth

"Growth is the great separator between those who succeed and those who do not. When I see a person beginning to separate themselves from the pack, it's almost always due to personal growth."

– John C. Maxwell

To grow is to expand, increase in size. It is a journey, a process that must be intentional; otherwise, it takes you nowhere.

To win in life and business, you must strategically have a growth plan for yourself. This plan must be in alignment with your mission, and move you towards your ultimate goal. For most people, the intention to start a new project is yearly, and perhaps that is what prompts the term and culture, New Year resolution. I want you to take a close look at your life, and have clarity of what matters most and where you are headed. Your growth plan may span monthly, quarterly, yearly, or even be suited to a particular season of your life.

It is beneficial to have a growth plan that is balanced and addresses many aspects of your life. To have a plan for your business and not have plans for your personal life and relationship does not make sense. Address all areas of your life; before you start, get a pen and paper and take inventory of yourself.

Take an inventory of your life. That means conducting a thorough assessment, with quantitative numbers, to identify where you need immediate action—raising the points and/or numbers, where applicable, will influence many other areas. I learned this the first time I had the privilege of working with a life coach. I had to look far and wide. I remember she called it a life wheel. I remember the analogy: If you have a flat tire in one area, it will cause your car to go slow, resulting in low efficiency. Some professionals will take you back in time to uncover areas that may be affecting your current growth. If you happen to have unpleasant experiences in your past—for example, a bad relationship—that might be the reason why you are unable to forge forward in your business. Setting a plan to address this area, perhaps healing and acquiring better tools through personal development, will then make you gain success. Personality tests like the DISC will help you uncover and appreciate your strengths. It is empowering to embrace your strengths when mapping out a growth plan, raising efficiency, and reducing frustration.

To succeed in life and business is to win. But to win, you need a strategy—a plan. Your plan must be very familiar to you, and you must become friends by all means. Succeeding is different for everyone. Therefore, own and believe in your plan.

"You must remain focused on your journey to greatness."

– Les Brown

If You Are Not Growing, You Are Dying

"It does not matter how slowly you go, as long as you do not stop."

– Confucius

The truth is that the Chinese bamboo tree never limited itself or played small in any way. It springs up and takes up space, spreading, and standing unapologetically. According to the story of the Chinese bamboo tree, it was a seed that took time to mature and absorb the necessary nutrients that were needed. The Chinese bamboo tree was not discouraged when the other trees grew. It did its work for five years. And in 6 short weeks, it grew 90 feet. I am telling you this because you are unique, and there is only one of you that is in existence, unless as science tells us, you have an identical twin. Comparing your trades and accomplishments with others will stunt your growth. Constant growth is the way to keep your dream and mission alive. If you are not continually adding to what you know, and not growing in any way, you are dying. Repeat, course correct if you must, but never stop becoming.

Your growth formula is particular to you. To be curious and choose to add to your current knowledge is a beautiful thing to do, and which you owe yourself. It becomes challenging when you were out of the formal educational system when expected to learn the material presented to you. Once out of formal education, please find a way to put learning into your daily routine.

In psychology, attaining mastery is a process. Tony Robbins calls this CANI: constant and never-ending improvement. You will first have the desire, and with every day, you get better. With repetition and the correct practice, you will get better, and your dream will come alive. What do you see when you watch a master perform on stage? I mean the stage of life or business. Magicians, speakers, singers, athletes, and other creatives have practiced and improved on their craft. I have noticed that they grow and add to the knowledge, which makes them acquire more fans. If you stop at anything, you will lose interest, and your craft becomes less appealing. I remember I loved to bake, and then I stopped trying, which made my dream diminish. I am a good cook today because I practice daily and have learned by experience; that is why I can automatically make up new recipes and innovations. You never have to be an expert to start. You make up your mind to begin, start with what you have, and with daily practice, you get better. If you are not continually growing, your dream or interest will die. Winning in life and business takes action and is a daily practice.

"It is from a small seed that the giant Iroko tree has its beginning."

– Nigerian Proverb

 Learn Something New Every Day

"If you want to earn more, learn more."

– Zig Ziglar

I was hoping you could add this to your daily routine. Wake up and decide what you want to learn for the day. But seriously, set a daily learning goal. Maybe call it a name, a fancy name—how about "Daily Pick-ups!" Hmm, that sounds fancy, but your nervous system registered it. As soon as you start your day, decide on what goes in your daily pick-up list. Keep it minimal. One a day is fine, but make it instinctual. Believe me, your subconscious knows what you are craving to learn; start there before overthinking. I know for sure, I need to learn how to change a tire on my car.

To be intentional with your learning is taking responsibility for your life. The good thing is that we now have more resources and information available than ever before. I mentioned earlier about my instincts, always letting me know that I needed to learn to change a tire. Suppose I followed through: I would have it on my list for the day, possibly research YouTube videos, read my car manual, and ask crucial questions. At the end of that day, I might have even tried to change one myself, which would open a whole new experience for me.

Next time you are going about your day, pay attention, and find out things that should make it on your daily pick-up list. Whatever sparks your interest—a life necessity or your curiosity—should make your list. If you find yourself questioning any situation, then you need to learn more about that. What new words did you hear? New York Times bestselling author, Raymond Aaron, who wrote the forward of this book you are now reading, says to find the meaning and etymology of a new word every day. How great it will be that you gain 365 new concepts a year.

Acquiring new knowledge will make you confident and better equipped to win in your life and business. You never know when you might need something, or perhaps when someone close to you needs it—wouldn't that be empowering to be informed? The most educated people are curious ones. I spent time with a friend that googled every occurrence in 3 hours. I had noticed that our conversation had stretched; her curiosity made me even more curious.

Another idea is to be an interviewer of people. Please quit talking about yourself; with every individual you come across, let it be about them—ask questions, and you will see yourself pulling knowledge. People naturally like to talk about themselves, so use this opportunity and let every encounter you have daily, teach you a thing or two.

To win at your life and business is a daily practice. It is the regular yearning to grow, to expand, and to be a lifelong learner.

"Learn from yesterday, live for today, hope for tomorrow. The most important thing is not to stop questioning."

– Albert Einstein

 Be the Dumbest Person in the Group

"When you talk, you are only repeating what you already know. But if you listen, you may learn something new."

– Dalai Lama

I have seen many successful people that are quiet and are not interested in unnecessary chatter. Perhaps you have been to a seminar or a conference, and you know the individual that always has something to say—she is the one that is always at the microphone. It is a good thing to share. However, I will still tell you that processing and assimilating information is also essential for your success. When you are the one doing all the talking, you are thinking of the next thing to say and, for the most part, are not listening. There is what we call active and passive listening. Next time you are in a conversation, listen to the verbal and non-verbal pause before you speak. Are you adding or clarifying? This will serve you well, as you can absorb and utilize information in a practical manner. Speak when you must, but never be the smartest in the room.

In business, always compliment yourself, meaning hire up when hiring associates or partners. Be intentional to hire someone better and more knowledgeable than you. If you are good at marketing, hire an expert in operations. Do not expect to be the most brilliant in your business by utilizing down, because you lose the advantage of adding value to your work. So always go for the best talents, both in life and industry.

If you are in a room and are the smartest person, you are limiting your growth because you are unable to expand to your full capacity. When you feel dumb, you are humbled, and only then do you get a chance to stretch out. The reason why playing a sport with people of a lower talent can be detrimental, is that you will play down, and by doing that, you never get challenged or improve on your skills. How about playing with superstars? This can be intimidating at first because it will expose your deficiency, and probably make you feel inadequate initially. With that, comes frustration, but that causes you to work harder to hone your skills so that you can keep up.

Success by no means requires growth, and for you to grow, you need to associate with people that are playing at a higher level, so you know what you do not know.

Only by doing this do you stand a chance to be the best at winning.

"You do not need to leave your room. Remain sitting at your table and listen. Do not even listen; simply wait, be quiet, still, and solitary. The world will freely offer itself to you to be unmasked. It has no choice; it will roll in ecstasy at your feet."

– Franz Kafka

Read; Be Diverse

"Reading is essential to those who seek to rise above the ordinary."

– Jim Rohn

Reading is the best gift to give yourself in order to foster your personal growth and development. There are many benefits of reading. The primary objective, we know, is to raise cognition. Reading also helps to curb stress and to make you more open-minded. You may not be able to have some experiences firsthand, but you can experience them through books. Books and reading can take you to faraway places, sparking your imagination. You can get lost in the characters, and might even experience some responses, like changing in a heartbeat, and even crying as the story unfolds. Reading biographies will help you understand real-life people's situations and experiences. Reading any non-fiction is about learning facts.

For you to be a winner in your life and business, you must be a person of authority or an expert in a given field. There is high confidence and respect for experts because you will believe that they are versatile; and overall, they know what they are doing. Opportunities will come to you. You will draw people to you. And suppose you are in business; you will attract quality customers that are willing to compensate for the time you have put into books. Confidence in any given subject comes with knowledge and experience. Reading can help you achieve that. My advice to you is that in whatever area of life and business, you make it a habit to be a student—read as many books as you can, and read far and wide to sharpen your knowledge.

Reading will make you adapt to many cultures and situations. Have you talked to someone lately that is a reader? Was there something different you noticed? Perhaps you saw their extensive vocabulary, their sincere interest, and their knowledge around several subjects of discussion. Reading will make you friendly because it will make you capable of participating in a vast topic of conversations, and that will boost your networking skills, creating new connections in your personal life and business.

Reading is a form of personal vacation, away from your current situation. Try a reading vacation. Or take a weekend off, stay home, turn off your phone, and read in an area of interest. You will appreciate this gift to yourself.

To win in your life and business, you must have the tools and a go-to place for your resources. When next you meet someone that is doing well, ask them what books they are reading. I usually will say, "What are you reading now?" Succeeding as a stay-home mother warrants that you gain skills and strategies to navigate the everyday challenges that come with managing a household. Winning in your business requires that you are knowledgeable or an expert in different aspects of running your business. Never give the excuse that you do not know something; find the book that has the answers you need, and win!

"If we encounter a man of rare intellect, we should ask him what books he reads."

– Ralph Waldo Emerson

Invest in Yourself

"Education is the key to unlock the golden door of freedom."

– George Washington Carver

Investing in yourself means that you value the potential and possibilities that lie within, and have decided to take steps to bring them alive!

Investing in yourself is non-negotiable if you want to move up in your life and business. I have never come across a successful person that is not actively engaged in self-improvement. You will see that as they are working on a project, they are simultaneously pursuing personal development. Education is essential, and so are learning new skills. There are many ways to invest in yourself. Travel, planned adventures and experiences, investing in a coach, attending seminars and workshops, reading educational books, and investing in your creativity are common ways. Formal education is pricey at every level. According to a recent survey, in 2018–2019, the average tuition for a college education was $35,676 at private colleges, and $9,716 at public institutions. So that means, for a four-year degree, you will invest about $142,704.00. If this wasn't important, do you think it would cost this much? You pay for formal education, with money and with time— lots of time! You will face the challenge of learning to pass a test.

Unfortunately, you spend time learning material of no interest to you. I believe my actual schooling started after my formal education. After my formal education, I decided which areas I wanted to develop, and the vehicles to use. Successful people will tell you that personal development comes after formal education.

Investing in yourself will make you confident because you will gain skills. Think of it like polishing a diamond; it shines brighter. You are investing in the best asset you have—yourself and your business. You get noticed and add value to all your associations. People will believe in you and what you have to say. You will learn new things, become an influencer, and will inspire and motivate people to take action and grow.

To not continually invest in your personal growth and development is to choose to die a premature death. It results in low self-esteem, a lack of self-fulfillment, and actualization. You can rightfully say that you are on this earth on a mission to find yourself. It should be a delightful adventure. Do not make it a waste of time, because you have only one chance to make it right. Choosing to enjoy this adventure and to give it all you got, making the best of yourself here on earth, is winning!

Investing in yourself is a sure way to add value and to increase profitability in your life and business. Everything you touch and associate with will turn to gold—your personal life, your family, and your business. Employers recognize this and will reward you through salaries and bonuses; your family will flourish, and you will build profitable companies.

"Intellectual growth should commence at birth and cease at death."

– Albert Einstein

MAIN TAKEAWAYS

Chapter 4: You Need A Mentor

Take a Look at Your Blind Spots

"I'm a mentor to anybody interested."

– Clint Eastwood

The area in which you fail to exercise judgement or discrimination make up your blind spot. Years ago, when I took the Landmark Forum, there were several distinctions taught at the forum. Still, the one that struck me most was that I have blind spots. Blind spots are areas in my life that I don't know; in other words, such regions are somewhat outside my awareness. Just like when backing up in a car, there are areas I do not see, and I need assistance or prompts to let me know what's in my way. I work with a mentor to uncover my blind spots and bring such areas to my attention. Insanity is doing the same thing over and over again and expecting a different result. I work with a mentor or a coach to get new tools and strategies to improve areas of my life and business. My mentors will boldly put me in the right spots.

Because this individual usually has more experience and/or is more knowledgeable, I save time, resources, and energy. Your mentors, especially, will hold you to a higher standard. My experience, though, is that you search diligently for the right fit for you, communicating your goals and staying authentic to who you are. I have found that well-informed coaches and mentors can be expensive since they will be spending their valuable time. You can start with group coaching and as you grow and became focused and intentional with your life, then make the necessary changes. Choose to invest in you. The highend coaches and mentors are not always the best and the most effective and may not be for you. Still, you may want to walk before you crawl, perhaps start small, and with time adjust accordingly. I have decided to be a winner, in all areas of my life and business. I prefer to have a guide while I do my work, and I encourage you to do the same.

"Insanity: doing the same thing over and over again and expecting different results."

– Unknown

Generating Leads and Ideas

"The best way a mentor can prepare another leader is to expose him or her to other great leaders."

– John C. Maxwell

I don't know what I don't know; for me to acquire new knowledge, and skills, I might hear, read, or watch. Because there is an abundance of resources nowadays, what happens is that I sometimes will have an information overload, where I are taking in way too much and are unable to process it, and therefore will not apply it. If you are familiar with this situation or have ever experienced it, your mentor or coach can help you here, in any specific area of your life; for example, public speaking, business development, and wealth building. Your coaches will give you the information on the specialized ideas that you need, saving you time so that you don't dive back into your habits of procrastination. Procrastination is to put off intentionally and habitually, to delay doing something until a later time because you do not want to do it. Ideas from books and media can be specialized info but sometimes may warrant sorting to get the right one. When you work with a mentor or coach, they may point you to specific books, contacts, seminars, masterminds, and conferences. I decided, in the past years, to always ask questions. Google searches are useful if you know what you are looking for, but that may still lead to confusion and procrastination. I have discovered that when I procrastinate, it is because I do not have the necessary information, or I lack clarity. So now, I do things differently, I ask myself some clarifying questions; what don't I understand, what questions should I be asking, and who should I be asking? I encourage you to try this practice. It will help to speed up your action like a winner.

"Bill Gates has always been a mentor and inspiration for me even before I knew him. Just growing up, I admired how Microsoft was mission focused."

– Mark Zuckerberg

The GPS

"A guru is like a live road map. If you want to walk uncharted terrain, I think it is sensible to walk on a road map."

– Jaggi Vasudev

Your mentor comes in your life when you need them. Your mentor has been through the same experiences that you are about to embark on. Qualified mentors are looking for you and want to direct you to your ultimate destinations. They can be a live GPS; A GPS according to the dictionary is a navigational system using satellite signals to fix the location of a radio receiver on or above the earth's surface. Your mentor will guide you; they may have been through the same situation; they know the roadblocks; they see the treasures before you.

If you're going from California to Seattle, you would want to put the address in the GPS. You will grab your key to start your car, and drive. You listen to the instruction of GPS lady or gentleman. On your way to Seattle, your GPS will tell you where to stop, how long a trip you have, weather conditions, and road closures; they should even provide alternative routes for you, so that you have a chance to make a decision. How awesome is that? The beauty of technology! Driving with GPS is a common practice all around the world. A friend once said to me, "I cannot live without my phone or GPS. I turn it on to go home from work." Wow! It is an autopilot—let someone think for you! I encourage you to be as dependent on a mentor as you are on your GPS, and you will be a winner in every area of your life. How about your goals and dreams? Imagine if you had a project to do. Before the project, you worked with a mentor, and you communicated your goals. Your mentor brings out your purpose, because sometimes it can be challenging to put your vision into words. Your mentor will hand you a road map. The road map will guide you to the quickest and fastest route to achieving your goals with less difficulty.

Most mentors and coaches are available and willing to adopt new protégés. But you must search for them. It might be as easy as asking someone—interview them, and ask if they are the right one for you. Or even better, "Are you available to mentor me?" Yes. It is that simple! I encourage you to do your research, and keep sorting; go with your heart, check in with your values, and always do what is best for you. Your mentor may be in a book. Many great teachers have put their wisdom in books.

Most people of influence, and wise leaders, need not be asked but are willing and available to guide you underneath their tutu ledge. Please take advantage of this opportunity when it opens up to you. It is a privilege.

"I think a role model is a mentor – someone you see on a daily basis, and you learn from."

– Denzel Washington

Waste No Time!

"The most significant difference is in the leadership. It was better for us. We had more coaches and mentors to help us. A lot of the young players today suffer from a lack of direction."

– Isaiah Thomas

When I set out to write this book, I had the goal of completing it at a definite time. I have heard of people that have completed books in 2 hours. Time is relative, and what makes time precious are the experiences and emotions that we associate with it. One thing is for sure; you have a definite time on earth, and every day that passes is gone! You can never turn the clock back. Minute by minute, it passes by.

In my early adult life, I have had a goal around fitness, finance, career, relationship, adventure, and fun. Some of those goals, I accomplished in a short time, while with some, I struggled perhaps with roadblocks, or maybe that goal wasn't as important to me. I am about to turn 50 years old in a few years, and have been inspired to write down 50 bucket lists items before this time. Turning 50 will come in 4 short years, so if I am committed to achieving my goals, I better seek mentors, coaches, and masterminds to guide me, so I waste no time. I encourage you, no matter how young you are, to treat time as a precious commodity. Save it, treasure it, and it will reward you.

"Time well-spent results in more money to spend, more money to save, and more time for a vacation."

– Zig Ziglar

Who Is Your Accountability Partner?

"If you have the resolution to go to the gym, it'll be a lot easier if you get a great trainer, or get your partner or your work buddy or your best friend to go with you so that you're held accountable to yourself and to that other person."

– David Kirsch

Accountability means to report and to remain obedient to a set plan. Your mentors will take responsibility and help you reach your goal because they want you to succeed. When I have to report to my mentor, I'm pushed to take action. Action creates momentum. Consistent effort, over time, will undoubtedly move me in the right direction. I am encouraging you to pay, and pay high fees, for your coaching, mentorship. Success for me always comes with a price, and the price usually is investing time, money, and the tenacity to follow through with all my obligations. A dream is nothing but a dream until you can turn your dream into a vision with a plan and action steps to get to a destination.

Another area that is powerful in accountability is think tanks and masterminds. This has become very popular these days because they produce results. I have noticed that masterminds have the ability to rally, encourage, and hold you accountable. In a genius group, you may also have people to mentor. Please do not take it lightly. The best way to grow is to teach. If you knew someone depended on you, wouldn't that make you want to improve yourself? On social media, there are groups and pages. Consider this your tribe; they are there to support and encourage, and truthfully, I have had many "aha" moments from social groups.

Some mentors and coaches are experts and authorities on specialized topics. Working with power is more bang for your buck. I assume they know the expectations in the area that you need help, and should make your journey and experience very pleasant. You benefit by branding yourself by association, because when you are mentored by an authority, you gain access to first-class information.

Now, prepare to mentor others.

"Starting a business is similar to an athletic endeavor, like serving a tennis ball. Telling you how to do it is useless. You get better through a combination of practice, coaching, and repetition, with money on the line."

– Andrew Yang

Who Is Your Role Model?

"I have to tell you. I'm the proudest of my life off the court. There will always be great basketball players who bounce that little round ball. Still, my proudest moments are affecting people's lives, effecting change, being a role model in the community."

– Magic Johnson

I saw Michelle Obama in 2019. After reading her books- Becoming, I had adopted her as a role model even before I set sight of her. Some of my mentors and role models are already dead, so I connect with them through books and their works. It is not uncommon in some cultures to believe in reincarnation of the reconnection with your past self. They are our role models, and a way to be inspired by your past experiences. I, too, believe in connecting with my ancestors. It is my intention always to make my ancestors proud.

My daughter was ten years old when she wrote a poem in school, describing her role model. I am her mother, but I never thought that she watched carefully. Because I am female and I'm the one closest to her, she admires my acts, my physicality, and overall, my personality. When she wrote the poem, she captured everything about me, from my daily habits and my practices to things that I didn't realize she was watching. She described my nail color, the color of my eyes, the texture of my hair and the composition of my skin. Wow! Such details. If I were to write a poem about my mother, I would also describe my mother with such information as she did.

Your role model is someone whose behavior you want to imitate. Your role model doesn't need to be someone older or more experienced. It is someone you like or have learned to love. I have adopted role models in my academic, professional, and spiritual life. I have noticed that some of my role models are not people that I am in contact with, or people that I even know or know me.

"As a parent, I have a job as a role model for my children, and by extension, to other young people."

– Kareem Abdul-Jabbar

MAIN TAKEAWAYS

Chapter 5: Optimal Health And Wellness

What's Up with Your Health?

"With age comes the understanding and appreciation of your most important asset, your health."

– Oprah Winfrey

You can live your best life if you are in good health. Life can be unkind when you do not have your health. Imagine waking up every day and your main task is to survive. To survive will become your primary goal. It is difficult to make a difference when not thriving. All your focus goes into the upkeep of your body. Scheduling doctor's visits and treatment plans will be your new to-do list. What it takes to stay up and about during the day can be overwhelming. How about you proactively plan and fill your calendar, to-do list, and schedule, with events that will feed your health.

Routine and timely visits with your health care professional is not an option. Make this a priority, and do not take it for granted just because perhaps you are pain-free or exhibiting no symptoms. You heal faster and, ultimately, when the disease is at the early stages. Since all the systems in the body and organs are interconnected, a disorder or malfunction in one will start to ooze and obstruct neighboring organs. Familiarize yourself with the timelines of all your routine visits. You stand a better chance at advocating for yourself when you are knowledgeable on the questions to ask when you get to your health care practitioner. Please be a student in this area. It pays a dividend. Symptom management is another area that you will need to pay attention to. There is no such thing as a not-so-severe symptom. Treat every symptom, from the common cold to the flu, a rash, or an insect bite, as something serious. I am not saying that you should be a hypochondriac, because you might be labeled and referred to a psychiatrist— another topic for another day. What I am saying is that suppose you have a cold; get advice, and treat it accordingly. I was perplexed when I heard that a sore throat could lead to kidney disease. So with anything, from skin problems to earaches, eye pain, allergic reactions, or unusual signs like hair loss, temperature changes should be discussed.

If you have a chronic disease like high blood pressure, diabetes, depression, or autoimmune diseases, daily checks on your vitals, and medication management, is a must. You will need to monitor your vitals. Perhaps you will need to frequently check your glucose, weight, blood pressure, INR, etc. Please get acquainted, and be an expert. Know your baselines, signs and symptoms, and red flags. Get prompt medical care as needed.

For you to function at your optimal health, it takes attention and practice to master the tasks needed in this area. To win in life and business requires that your health is in check. After all, your whole life, in general, revolves around your health. It is a miserable life to have ill health, and business will go wrong! Decide to be a winner— your health matters.

"To keep the body in good health is a duty…otherwise, we shall not be able to keep our mind strong and clear."

– Buddha

 Break a Sweat

"If we could give every individual the right amount of nourishment and exercise, not too little and not too much, we would have found the safest way to health."

– Hippocrates

Physical activity in any form is a normal process and is vital for your health and wellness. You may commonly relate exercise with the strenuous activity of something unpleasant, or you may love it. It all depends on your orientation. To push yourself to break a sweat may, in fact, be the easiest way to get your exercise accomplished. Sweat is caused by perspiration. Sweat will cool your body down, promote heart health, and detoxify the body of heavy metals and toxins.

You will notice that when you embark on an exercise, maybe a walk or run, the best indicator to self-monitor is by your sweat. As soon as you sweat, there is an increase in energy, you feel more relaxed, the temperature cools, and your mood changes. I encourage you to break a sweat, and every day. If you have access to a sauna or steam room, that's another way to sweat, as it will give somewhat same benefits as with exercise. What if you have a time of day that you hold yourself accountable for breaking a sweat? Or even regularly use it as a go-to modality for treating or turning around your everyday predicaments, like making critical decisions, tackling your crucial task for the day, mood swings, or fatigue. What I am saying is that if you form the habit of incorporating sweating in your daily routine, it will make a tremendous difference in how you function.

Stress will be the most common cause of burnout and overwhelm in your life and business. The fact is that there is no perfect life, and I haven't heard of anyone that does not have challenges every now and then. This is the reason why the most successful people in the world start their day with physical exercise. When you start your day with physical activity, you are deliberately putting gas in your tank. You will have a reserve for the day and will be able to handle any challenges. You will be better equipped to make the right decisions, and you are more alert. You will reduce stress and anxiety in your life.

I encourage you to think of exercise as medicine. Any continuous movement will stimulate your body, causing you to sweat, and will be helpful for the maintenance and upkeep of your body and mind.

"Exercise is really important to me; it's therapeutic. So if I'm ever feeling tense or stressed or like I'm about to have a meltdown, I'll put on my iPod and head to the gym or out on a bike ride along Lake Michigan with the girls."

– Michelle Obama

Nature and All the Benefits

"Look deep into nature, and then you will understand everything better."

– Albert Einstein

According to the dictionary, nature is the creative and controlling force in the universe. It is all the animals, plants, and other things in the world that are not made by people, and all the events and processes that are not caused by people. It is the form of existence for all things. You cannot talk about health and wellness without mentioning the significant role of nature in your reality. Therefore, it is the essence of who you are.

When I take an early morning walk, everything is quiet everywhere. I see the magnificence of nature. I also observe nature when I visit select destinations like the Grand Canyon, a safari, and oceans around the world. There is a stillness that lets me know that they are in charge.

Mother Nature is indeed bigger than life. It is a beautiful thing to know and believe that there is a force greater than you are, and to acknowledge it and let it show you its beauty and healing.

There are many benefits of nature, and you probably will agree with me. The air you breathe, as simple and how readily available it is to you, is nature at work. I encourage you to acknowledge all the help it gives you, and to be thankful. I, for sure, know that life is more prominent than I can ever imagine; I realize its intelligence and power. There is healing, peace, harmony, creativity, and strength—and the list can go on and on. To surrender to this power, and knowing that it is infinite, is liberating. You will wonder at the sunsets, sunrises, waterfalls, and oceans, because you do not understand it completely, although science will explain it to an extent. When you are on a beach vacation and have no company, the water is there with you, and nature will remind you that you are infinite. There is a rejuvenation that comes in connecting with nature; hence, the nature walk. When you take a nature walk or vacation in natural environments, you are seeking to reconnect with that which is higher and more prominent than you are. You will be nourished and refreshed; as a result, it is just a gentle reminder of how helpless you can be. You need nature.

Nature is readily available to you. You do not need to take a vacation or travel afar to find her. Observe the still night, watch a bird or an animal—I encourage you to seek out ways in which you are regularly connected with nature, tie that with your daily agenda to feed your soul, and be alive. It will calm you and boost creativity. You will hear yourself, as ideas will pop into your head, and it will sharpen you and make you younger. Try this, and you will continue to win in a wholesome way!

"All water has a perfect memory and is forever trying to get back to where it was."

– Toni Morrison

Nutrition

"At the most elite level, your nutrition becomes a lifestyle: it's not something you have to do when you're preparing for Olympic games or World Cup games—you just do it. You're more inclined to eat healthier because it's better for your muscles."

– Abby Wambach

Your body is your temple. Your body is a machine, driving you to your desired destinations in life and business. Your body needs an adequate supply of fuel for it to run at its optimal level. Nutrition plays a crucial role in your overall health. Food and/or nutrition is an act or process of nourishing or being nourished, a science that interprets the nutrients and other substances in food concerning maintenance, growth, reproduction, health, and disease. Your diet will determine your nutrition or the nourishment that you receive.

Your diet is vital and requires diligence on your part. Proper education and continued research for information and knowledge are essential, but the good news is that the building blocks are all the same. You need adequate quantity and the right quality of carbohydrates, proteins, fats, vitamins, and minerals to be up and going; otherwise, you may be malnourished and will require medical intervention. If you can keep your diet simple for the most part, please do so, as you will have better control of what you are consuming. When you are in a grocery store, fresh broccoli and canned, processed broccoli are two different items. Also, broccoli from a local farmers market will be different from the one from out of state and sometimes even from across countries. The less processed and local foods are always better.

Choose wisely. Be meticulous about getting the right fuel and in the right combinations. With proper nourishment, you have energy, strength, and stamina to thrive, and a healthy body is a very fit body. Diseases and ailments are kept away.

I encourage you to keep a food diary to capture your nutrient intake, as well as the quality. If you have chronic conditions like high blood pressure, diabetes, or some autoimmune disease, avoiding some food may be beneficial, providing healing effects. Do your research, and find out which eating style is the best for your body type, metabolism, or even lifestyle.

Consulting with a nutritionist or also taking cooking classes is something to consider. When you get the best tools, you are empowered and, therefore, can make the right choices for yourself. To overeat is not a way of proper nutrition; take in the adequate micro/macro amount to provide the cells in your body the building blocks it needs. If you can master this area of your health, then you are doing better than most. Keep working at it until you get the results you want. To win in this area is critical.

"I look at how my kids view exercise. They have a complete understanding that nutrition and exercise go hand in hand. I didn't think like that when I was a kid, but they have a real consciousness about it that I'd like to think comes from the years of attention we've put into this."

– Michelle Obama

Yoga

"The meaning of yoga is connection of mind, body, and spirit. If you have a bad telecommunication system, your body gets sick. Yoga helps fix that."

– Bikram Choudhury

Like many, you would associate yoga as a system with physical postures, breathing techniques, and meditation, and one which is completed independently. My experience with yoga changed as I discovered it for myself for over three years. I was motivated to try yoga, seeking the postural and stretching properties that it promised. I now understand yoga to mean a philosophy teaching suppression of all activity of body, mind, and will, so that the self can realize its distinction and attain liberation. Yoga is a way of life. A novice will say "I do yoga," and will state the physical properties, but a yogi says "practice," and describes a state of being.

Yoga is a beautiful practice for anyone, especially if you are looking for a way to look inwards. It has many healing qualities, and when you start to practice yoga, quieting your mind might be the most challenging piece. Do not worry; it may take you a few times to understand what this even means. Introspection is a gift in itself, because you are believing and trusting yourself to seek inwards where all your answers are. Also, you will get other benefits like increased muscle strength, increased energy levels, improved respiration, weight loss, a balanced metabolism, improved circulation, injury protection, and better performance and stress management. When I practice yoga, I notice that I am mindful, can ease into movements and postures, and am in synchrony with my breathing. With yoga, I see a difference in my attitude, and I sleep better. I also have a healthy appetite. Yoga and meditation will help you to be centered. Your creativity will flow. You will become the better version of yourself and will be available to make a difference in your life and business.

I encourage you to find a practice that works for you. Although the philosophy is the same, there are different modes of practice. I loved Bikram Yoga. It stretches my physical body out to a point that I feel the lengthening from the inside out. There is a therapeutic effect since you are in a hot room. It is meditation. It will force you to stay with yourself for 90 minutes, with the intensity, focus, and concentration to maintain the various postures. Sprinkle yoga in your life. Breathe, pay attention to your body, spend time alone, and this may be the key to your stress-free experiences.

"Become slower in your journey through life. Practice yoga and meditation if you suffer from 'hurry sickness.' Become more introspective by visiting quiet places such as churches, mountains, and lakes. Give yourself permission to read at least one novel a month for pleasure."

– Wayne Dyer

Endurance

"The winners in life treat their body as if it were a magnificent spacecraft that gives them the finest transportation and endurance for their lives."

– Denis Waitley

To endure means to persist in spite of hardship. Physical endurance is the ability to sustain a prolonged stressful effort or activity, as you see with a marathon runner that endures over 25 miles of a road race. To complete a run, the runner completes a level of training and, of course, has the commitment to train and finish the race. There are many benefits of endurance training and conditioning; amongst these are a healthier body, clearer thinking, better self-image, confidence, peace of mind, more energy, better sleep, youthfulness, and overall better quality of life. Endurance builds up over time since your body adapts to the workload. You are training the aerobic system of your body. There are specific guidelines and protocols to endurance training as it relates to sports, and I encourage you to seek the advice of a professional trainer.

There are two ways I look at endurance as it relates to the topic of discussion in this book: physical endurance, like you would see in a marathon runner or soccer player; and the will of an individual to persist and turn hardship into glory. There is a resolve to finish, which is what you will find with these two scenarios mentioned. For you to handle the ups and downs in your life and business, you need some grit to be able to tolerate the not so favorable conditions as you get to the finish line in your endeavors. One of the best realizations you will have is to take life and business as a marathon. Think long term, and always prepare for the difficulties; pace yourself through such things, and still stay on track.

I encourage you to be intentional about building physical aerobic capacity, to carry over to your results. I once asked a runner why she does races all the time, and she said that the discipline that she applies, to train for the events, carries over to her life and helps her with her business. And another friend jokes that she will prepare all year round in case there is a need to run from a lion; she could beat the beast and help everyone escape. To be prepared to win also means that you are already a winner. Get ready, get fit, train for it, and victory is yours.

"Being a winger or a wide mid, I have to run continuously for 90 minutes, which not only takes endurance but also strength in my legs to be able to be explosive for 90 minutes. I think weight training has really allowed me to sustain for those 90 minutes."

– Megan Rapinoe

MAIN TAKEAWAYS

Chapter 6: Your Support Groups And Communities

Inner Circle/Your Internal 5

"You will never outperform your inner circle."

– John Wooden

You will have around 5 people in your life that you are never in competition with. They may not be family as this is what most will associate with closeness, or they might have been long adopted into your life as a family. These individuals are not necessarily those that you socialize with or are seen with all the time. They are your innercircle people, who not only know you but appreciate, respect, and value your goals and aspirations. They hear your silence, and even from a distance, they can recognize your desires and wishes.

The people that are most commonly in your inner circle are family, mentors, coaches, spouses, and best friends—commonly the people you have a history with, who have known you for quite a while. It is not uncommon to see that amongst this group of individuals; they are the ones that will actively help forge you on to your destinations. You will have a wise one, a truth-teller, who will be calling out your bullshit. There should be an encourager and not an enabler. They care and will hold you accountable. There may be an expert here who may be a mentor, and then one genius member that will be thinking on her feet.

I encourage you to make a list of 3–5 people that are in your inner circle. If you do not have them identified, it is time to begin recruiting. Who will you call when you get the best news of your life, or when you hit rock bottom, and the world is crumbling down on you? Who would be your last call if you were to make the ultimate decision on your life? These questions should give you an idea of how big and full this list should be. Do not feel bad if the person dearest to you does not make this list; but those that make it to your inner circle must recognize that they are members of your inner circle, and acknowledge that. For the most part, you will be a member of their inner circle, too, and if not, do not worry about it—as I said, you are never in competition with these fellows.

Life and business are a journey, with a destination and a vision; but what I know for sure is that it is never a smooth ride. That is why I call it a roller coaster ride; there are unique challenges and triumphs. You must have a specialized team of counselors and supporters who can hold you accountable while on this trip. It is, therefore, necessary to have a high standard for your inner circle.

"He who loves 50 people has 50 woes; he who loves no one has no woes."

– Buddha

Your Community

"People who work together will win, whether it be against complex football defenses or the problems of modern society."

– Vince Lombardi

There is a group in which you will typically find yourself in many areas of your life. In this place, you will notice that although sometimes you are not in close contact with the people, you are unable to function independently from this group of individuals. It is called community. A community is a group of people that are bound together by interests or location. According to the dictionary, it is a unified body of individuals, such as people with common interests living in a particular area; groups of people with a common characteristic or interest, living together within a society (for example, a retirement community or an academic community). Some synonyms include clan, clique, network, set, and body. Members of your professions—religious, political, sports, the schools—are examples of your community. I encourage you to pay attention to the various groups that you are involved in, and to the members and the mission of the group. You are unable to climb greater heights in your personal life and business without the input of society. This group will directly or indirectly affect your outcome in any situation. Nurture your community, get involved, and know the makeup and details. Know where you are needed and the value you can add, and never hesitate to do your part.

There are benefits when you are a part of a community; the connections you make will improve your personal and your work life. You never know what individuals you will meet and who they will know. There is a lot of inspiration from a community. Being part of a group will help open up your imagination as you will come across new ideas. There are resources and further information that may lead you to achieve your goals and dreams, available to you when you are around a diverse group. There can be support, as in referrals to your ventures. Your city is where people will help you sell your ideas and your business.

In some communities, you are automatically enrolled and are obligated to be part of it, like your neighborhood— you live there, so you are therefore a member. In other instances, you do not live in close locations but are linked due to a common interest. I encourage you to build your society, decide which circles you want to move in, find ways to be a part of it, and add value. Hence, people join social clubs, gyms, and charities. The investment in time and effort is worth it. Build for yourself one community at a time, where you get to contribute and serve. You will notice that you will be supported, celebrated, inspired, and connected.

"Alone, we can do so little; together, we can do so much."

– Helen Keller

Family Circles

"A happy family is but an earlier heaven."

– George Bernard Shaw

Family is the primary unit where you began your existence. It gives you your first identity and security. The family will typically be made up of parents and members of the same ancestry. The essential constituent of the society traditionally consists of two parents rearing their children. The family makeup is different for many. I know people that have had the privilege to choose their own family, with no shared genetics. Whatever family means to you, you will agree that family is the primary source of life and connection to the creator.

If you are like most people, you are in close contact with family, and are perhaps able to maintain a good positive relationship. But the circumstances are different for many that have less than ideal situations. When one hurts or rejoices in a family group, it will spread and affect many (e.g., the birth or death of a family member). Hence, the famous sayings: "There is strength in family," and "Family is everything." I believe your family, by all means, are your appointed social circle by the creator, packaged to teach and equip you to face the world. You do not choose your family; it is God's gift to you as you are to them.

Like I mentioned before, a traditional family will consist of 2 parents rearing their children. Also, there are various social units differing from but regarded as equivalent to the traditional family (e.g., a single parent family, and other forms of non-traditional families). That shows that what you want primarily as a human is the interconnectedness, love, and security that the family unit promises. It would be best if you nurtured what was given to you, and make an effort to build your family on a solid foundation. You will be happy you did that, so that when the storms of life happen, you have shade, and you will also have people to rejoice with. Put in the work so that you can reap the benefits that come from having a family. These benefits include higher self-esteem, happy memories, love, and acceptance. It includes social time, practicing gratitude and forgiveness, and accepting others since you do not get to choose your own family. Your family will push you; love them anyway. There is a thing called sibling rivalry. Your biggest competition might be family; it isn't uncommon. The family will strengthen your social and emotional muscles to be equipped to handle the outside world.

To do well in life and business, family is essential. With a stable and happy family, you have fewer stresses and are able to focus on your mission. When there is stress in the family, it affects all that you do, leading to unproductivity. Please choose to win by making family a priority.

"To us, family means putting your arms around each other and being there."

– Barbara Bush

YOU

"I am just one human being."

– Dalai Lama

You are your own best friend—before you can form a relationship with others, it is better to have one with yourself! There is no other source that knows you better than you know yourself. You, thee, thou, your, and ye are often referred to by spiritual leaders as the spirit within. To know thyself, and appreciate yourself as a friend, there has to be a deep connection with self and love, to be able to spend quality time on your own.

You are the primary source, the source and origin of all your social circles. A good sense of self helps you to create an even better relationship and support from the outside. When you support and encourage yourself, others will support and assist you. You will build strong bonds and connections when you have a real sense of self. People will treat you accurately as you treat yourself, or at least close to how you see yourself.

I encourage you to get familiar with yourself. You can uncover your truth by asking your deep self-questions, writing in your journal, and being transparent. Some common questions are: Who are you? What do you stand for? What are you passionate about? What are your values, and what is your mission? When you know yourself, you do not have to prove yourself—you are happy, and you enjoy time with yourself, with your family, your inner circle, and your community. You will also feel better about sharing yourself and your values with the world.

I typically find that people that are hard and unkind to themselves often tend to attract the same kinds of individuals. When you learn to cultivate self-love, you will love and cherish yourself. You will set boundaries with yourself. Introverts know this too well—the need to recharge and regroup before dealing with other people. If you maintain this common practice of going into the self to seek answers, you will endure many benefits of self-love and acceptance. There is a greater awareness that can be cultivated, but it takes trust with self. When you have a good relationship with YOU, you will get more things done, because since you trust yourself, you get to make quick decisions. You will also be a good friend and be very pleasant to hang around, which is a gift to everyone. And as you get better at knowing yourself and having a good relationship, you will notice that you will miss yourself when you are gone a lot— when this happens to you, it is a good sign.

"It is better to conquer yourself than to win a thousand battles. Then the victory is yours. It cannot be taken from you, not by angels or by demons, heaven, or hell."

– Buddha

Which Other People?

"We all need people who will give us feedback. That's how we improve."

– Bill Gates

There is another exceptional group of people that you will have in your social circle, called the "other people." These other people are those that you don't know—those people that you meet on the bus, at the airport, at the museum, or on your commute in traffic—you will meet them in far and near places. You do not know and perhaps will only see them once in your life. You may never even interact with them, but they remain present in your life. They are the ones at the beach judging everyone. They may be the ones that will even give feedback when you attend to them in stores or in other services that you may be involved in.

You see, the reason why you can never ignore this group is that you will need them in your everyday operation. You need skills to mingle, engage, and interact with them, since they do not know you. The first impression always works with these individuals—think eye contact, a smile, body language, patience, and simple courtesy. You get maybe one chance alone to impress them, and yet their opinion will matter and will go far. That new promotion, bonus, and business referral may be due to the influence of your "other people." They may have had good experiences with you when they met you at the airport or at the mall.

I want you to pay attention to how you conduct yourself in your personal life and business. Be kind to people. You will continue to recruit your community, inner circles, and even family from your other people, so keep sifting; it's an ongoing project. In this group, you will find your partner in life and business. Think about spouses that met on a cruise to Alaska because the man was polite and let his future bride get in line. That is how life works; everyone you meet is vital and has a direct impact to you your affairs.

The other people in your life, though, who are not your friends or inner circle, are the ones that will determine your character and integrity. You will assume that because you don't know them personally or in business, they do not matter, but that's not true. According to Malcolm S. Forbes, you can easily judge the character of a man by how he treats those who can do nothing for him. Noticing how you interact with your other people will be an excellent way to get genuine feedback per area that needs improvement in your social and emotional skills. It is also a great way to find talents for your businesses and future partnerships in your work and industry.

"Pretend that every single person you meet has a sign around his or her neck that says, 'Make me feel important.' Not only will you succeed in sales, you will succeed in life."

– Mary Kay Ash

 Social Media

"People often say that motivation doesn't last. Well, neither does bathing—that's why we recommend it daily."

– Zig Ziglar

Social media has come to stay, and there has been a shift in the way people view its contributions. If you were born in the last decade, you were born into the social media age, and it makes up a big part of your social group. The younger generation will see it as a way of life, while the older folks may see it as a chore or distraction. Still, either way, I have not seen any individual lately that has not done anything or has not been impacted by social media.

In this chapter, I have discussed different social groups. Social media can be the glue that binds the various groups. Since you now live in the information age, where you carry your life in your hand, aka the cell phone, you have ready access to your social circles. To reach out to anyone that you have called a friend, is easy. There are different platforms for social media. You may like Facebook, while others, especially the millennials, like Instagram. There is also LinkedIn for the professional communities. Information is shared faster, and you can get quick updates about members of your social circle. Collaboration is more efficient; you are never alone if you choose to embrace social media.

To have a business and not be on social media is insanity, and even in your personal life, as you will be denying yourself of the many perks. Social media will help you build a network and community fast, as you can reach a broader range of people. Branding, marketing, and staying on top of your product are other advantages. Social media will help boost your visibility; you can stay on top of industry news, and learn more about your social circles. One thing I have learned in the past few years is that if you are responsible, social media makes it easy to encourage self and business—you can share insights and grow all around. I have seen great companies come out of social media, and partnerships that started on social media.

I suggest getting familiar with this fantastic tool. Choose the platform that works best for you, based on preferences. Social media is userfriendly for the most part. You might find that when using it on a more enormous scope in business, you may require additional training. Support is available and has no cost. The days of ignoring social media are over. Use it to get visible, build a network, build community, connect with family, and to get quick access to those that matter most in your life, business—and win!

You Are a Liar (A Measly Little Liar)

"I'm fine". "I'm doing well." "My day's been good." You are a fucking liar. You know that is a lie and you say it anyway. You are lying everyday. You lie to your family, your partner, your friends, and yourself. You lie to yourself all the damn time. Each and every day. Okay, what exactly is lying? Obviously if you understand the meaning of English words then you know what lying is and what it means. You are saying something that isn't true. Most people think lying is bad or frowned upon, although, most people can also agree that lies which do not create any real problems are insignificant. For example, "I'm fine", "I'm doing well", and "my day has been good". Now you may have been having a good day and you may be doing well, but let's be honest, you have said this shit before when it hasn't been true at all. Let's call these little white lies. Little white lies are considered insignificant and justified. So why do we say these white lies? Well it's simple. We literally couldn't give two fucks about explaining how our day is, how we are doing, and how this is, and blah blah blah.....The second you actually say, "My day hasn't been going well" or "I'm not doing well", you know there is a chance you will get sucked into a conversation that doesn't help you. This DOES NOT just go for these statements. Sometimes you just don't want to talk about something with someone else because it is simply a waste of time. NOW, it is important to talk about things and you know that. If you really are having a bad day and you aren't doing well, many people find it beneficial to just talk to someone about it. Obviously if there is a real problem or situation that is making your day bad or making you feel unhappy or not well, you need to attack that issue and solve that problem immediately. Sometimes "talking about it" doesn't do shit and you need to DO something about it. ANYWAYS. You say little white lies all the time, it doesn't matter, don't worry about it. You say these things because you have a life, you have things to do, you have an agenda, and sometimes you don't want to explain how things are and how you are doing because it isn't going to get you anywhere. I hope that now you have an understanding of the difference between lying and white lies. Because there is a difference and anyone who says "YOU CAN NEVER LIE, IT CREATES A BAD MINDSET AND WILL HINDER YOUR ABILITY TO ACHIEVE GREATNESS" is a dumbass and they probably lie a lot. So now that we got white lies out of the way, what about lies that matter? Lies that are kind of a big deal. Here are some examples: Lying to your significant other about what you are doing (like if you know you are doing something wrong and your significant other would definitely think it's wrong),

122

lying to your business partners/customers, and basically just lying about shit that has significant consequences. Now you should never lie about things that matter because then problems arise. I would say most lies happen in relationships. You may lie to your significant other because you don't love them anymore, maybe you despise them, or that you just don't like them. You lie because you are afraid of losing that person and ending a relationship. Lying tends to happen because you are avoiding a PROBLEM. There SHOULDN'T EVEN BE A PROBLEM. If you have to lie, and I mean actually lie about shit that matters. Like how you feel about someone or something similar to that, there is a real issue. Why is that an issue? Because if you are in a stale relationship or with a fucking toxic human being, or someone who is annoying, controlling, obsessive, hateful, rude, disrespecful, ect; If you lie to keep that relationship going, then you ARE A

SAD HUMAN BEING. GET YOURSELF TOGETHER. SLAP YOURSELF IN THE FUCKING FACE BECAUSE YOU NEED TO GET OUT OF THAT HELLHOLE AND QUIT THE ENDLESS CYCLE OF BULLSHIT. Even if this person is okay sometimes or even if they are amazing here and there, you need to figure out if these nice little moments are worth the continuation of a relationship that may be making your life miserable. Even if this person is the best thing that has ever happened to you, look at the negative parts of the relationship. Understand what is really going on in your relationship and what this person is doing to you. how are they changing you and how are they affecting your life. You may not even realize you are changing into a person you don't want to be.This is when people lie. They are afraid to lose a relationship that is good enough to make them not feel lonely, depressed, and stuff like that. THERE IS THE PROBLEM. You cannot settle for a shit relationship that has some good in it or even a lot of good in it. Instead, end a garbage relationship instead of lying to yourself and to your partner because you are dependent on an endless cycle of BULLSHIT. You would rather deal with dumb problems everyday instead of actually trying to grow as a human being. When you have to lie to yourself and to someone else everyday in order to keep something going then that mindset will seep into your life, into the decisions you make, and inhibit you from becoming a fucking BEAST. This type of lying makes you feel comfortable where you are. It's a cycle. If you are in a toxic relationship, it seems like the same issues keep resurfacing over and over and over and over again. That's because just like how you are continuously lying in order to keep a pathetic relationship going, you are continuously having to deal with the same problems that take up mental energy and simply make your life less enjoyable. If you are in a happy, healthy relationship then that is obviously a great thing and keep that going for as long as you can. SO WHAT HAVE WE LEARNED? Little white lies are okay. Lies that you know are bad and especially the ones that keep a shitty relationship going, need to stop right now. In fact, I'll wait. Seriously, if you are in a bad relationship right now or if there is any lie that you have been continuing in order to avoid an issue or avoid a difficult situation, I will wait until you do what you need to do. DO WHAT NEEDS TO BE DONE. Please, for yourself. I am here to guide you and help you create a happier, lighter, and more beautiful life that is not butchered and fucked up by an endless cycle of lies and bullshit. I am begging you to speak the full truth to whoever needs to hear it. THIS DOESN'T just go for people in relationships. STOP LYING TO YOURSELF. If you are single and maybe you have gone through a shitty relationship and you had to end it. Good fucking job. That is hard to do. That is an accomplishment and I am fucking proud of you. High five*. And maybe someone broke up with you. That is also just as difficult to deal with, maybe even more difficult then breaking up with someone else. Especially things like ending marriages and getting divorced, those are serious situations and they are hard to deal with. You may be heartbroken, sad, whatever it is. BUT GUESS WHAT? You are a free flying human that can accomplish anything and now you aren't hindered by someone else. If you are a super dependant person, and you can't function without someone else, grow some fucking balls. The most important thing in life is being happy with just yourself, your abilities, and who you are as a person. Relationships can be fucking delightful. What is the formula for a beautiful relationship? Two amazing human beings who can function in life without leeching off of other people's energy. That is literally all you need. And obviously some love and trust.

How to Become Healthier Permanently

Let's transition from relationship stuff over to other challenges that are being avoided by lying. Are you fat? Are you unhealthy? Are you depressed, anxious, socially inadequate? Are you dumb? You can't accomplish things like other people can? Maybe you feel behind? Yeah, whatever negative thought is bouncing around in the back of your brain, it probably has some truth to it. Maybe that thought has a lot more truth to it than you might think. Let's attack some of these thoughts you have, one by one. Let's start with thoughts about your physical health. Listen, you may be unhealthy. You don't just have to be fat to be unhealthy by the way. Everyday, thoughts about your physical health cross your mind. Even if you are shredded with five percent body fat, you think about your physical health. Even healthy average joes who are happy with their body think about their physical health daily. These thoughts contribute to eating well, working out, staying fit, and all the other stuff that contributes to being healthy. The thing is, if you are not physically healthy, thoughts about your physical health are probably negative. STOP BEING UNHEALTHY. STOP. RIGHT NOW. Eat healthier, exercise more, and figure out how to be healthier in general. Look shit up on Google. The healthier you are, physically and mentally, the happier you are. You may know that you need to make physical changes in order to become healthier but maybe you keep trying and then giving up. Or maybe you haven't even tried at all. This is because you don't have the willpower to make that decision in order to change your life for the better. It takes forever to get shredded or to be a super healthy human being. So it makes sense that people give up. Because it's hard to do. You may lie to yourself without even knowing it when it comes to your physical health. You may know that you have health problems but you are stuck in this cycle of either not making an effort to become healthy or trying to become healthy and then just giving up. This is a form of lying to yourself. Your mind, instead of pushing you everyday to become better and healthier, it doesn't. This happens because you are used to where you are in life, physically and mentally, and your mind does not care to change. After all, you are alive where you are now and your brain is cool with that. It just wants to live. TAKE CONTROL OF YOURSELF. CHANGE YOUR MINDSET. When you are giving up on your physical goals, the moment before you give up, your brain makes that decision. You weigh the positives and negatives and unfortunately, your brain tells you that there is more of a benefit to stop this fitness journey versus continuing that journey. TRAIN YOUR BRAIN. To do this, you simply push yourself when you feel like quitting. Yeah, I know how generic that sounds and it's 100 percent accurate. And it will change your life and make you healthier. SO, what about other thoughts? Being physically healthy plays a HUGE role in your mental health and you already knew that. But what if you are experiencing other issues. Issues that may not be related to your physical health. ANXIETY AND DEPRESSION. Yes, the two accomplices that are guilty of completely ruining peoples' lives. There is a reason for your anxiety and depression. It could be something you need to change physically and/or mentally. People who are overweight and unhealthy tend to have a higher chance of being depressed and anxious. Is that the problem you have? Or is it something else? You may be depressed because of genetics and you may be anxious because of the same reason. There could be a chemical unbalance in your body that causes you to feel these ways. Honestly, it's hard to pinpoint the exact reason why you feel certain ways. You have the entire internet to help you. You can research dietary supplements, herbs, and things like that to help eliminate anxiety and depression. Also working out, being social, doing shit, and talking to someone about your issues will benefit you. It's great to try to solve things yourself and try to eliminate mental issues by yourself. It can happen but sometimes you just need someone else. If you really try your best to take care of your mental health and just can't seem to pinpoint the cause of the issue, just talk to a doctor. A lot of people are nervous and hesitant to talk to a doctor about mental health issues and it makes sense. You may be embarrassed, self conscious, and closed off about your problem. DOCTORS ARE THERE TO HELP YOU. Never ever let your negative thoughts keep you from finding help. You only have this one life and you have to make this life beautiful. So, talking to a doctor might be what you need to do and please just do it, don't hesitate, don't be afraid, they want to help you and make your life better. ALTHOUGH, I do believe anxiety and depression can be cured by simply training your mind, creating a healthy and balanced lifestyle, as well as being more social. The more amazing things happening in your life, the busier your mind will be. A lot of times anxiety and depression come from overthinking things and just being stuck in your head all day. Once again, you may be in a cycle and to end this cycle YOU NEED TO MAKE A CHANGE. Anything that will make you truly happier won't necessarily be easy - it takes effort. Make an effort to change yourself for the better and make yourself happier. It is strange that finding happiness and being content tends to always be on the other side of a challenge that you must face and endure. That is the beauty of life. There are challenges and challenges are hard but getting past that difficulty always feels so rewarding and it really can change your life, if you just try. A big problem is lying to yourself when you know you have physical or mental problems. Telling yourself, "I'm fine", when really you aren't and you know you aren't but you are alive and your mind will tell you anything in order for you to stay where you are mentally and physically. Like I said before, your mind knows you are living and thinks that whatever you have done so far, it's worked because you aren't dead. This is a pre-historic mindset which everyone has. There is a reason why you don't feel motivated and excited to face new challenges that will benefit your life. So basically, humans first appeared in Africa a very long time ago. Most of the fossils from the earliest humans range from 6 to 2 million years old. Now it's been a long time since then. Back then, humans were fighting fucking animals up close, living with no technology at all, and just surviving off of anything they could. It was fucking primal back then (obiously). Many primal instincts remain in humans today. The most common one being: Wanting to fuck people. If you are just a regular teenager, young adult, or just any adult, you are horny. Anywhere you go, thoughts about having sex creep into your mind. These urges are strong and that's because your body LOVES LIFE. For some reason your brain wants your body to reproduce. Living things have a fucking obsession about life and living. It's beautiful. In our world today, everything is so fucking easy. I know there are many people who are unlucky, have a shitty life, and have to deal with a lot of bullshit. But hopefully most of you have a pretty good life and don't have to deal with too many major problems. Because living nowadays is much easier than before, it is easy to become extremely comfortable with your life. Even if you have a lot of problems. What I'm getting at here is that your brain, considering it loves life, wants you to live. That is why you don't have the willpower and motivation to change yourself for the better. Your primal instincts make you feel comfortable where you are in life. EVEN IF YOU THINK THAT YOU HAVE GIVEN IT YOUR ALL, you probably haven't. TRAIN YOUR MOTHER FUCKING BRAIN. I keep saying, "your body and your brain". Remember, you are one entity. Your brain and body is one. Negative thoughts are coming from YOU. Remember that you are yourself, so don't let yourself talk you out of things or make you unhappy and unmotivated. It takes effort to make changes in your life. I have said that now like a thousand times. MOST OF YOU KNOW WHAT YOU NEED TO DO TO CHANGE YOUR LIFE FOR THE BETTER so JUST DO IT. You know what I'm saying? STOP telling yourself that everything is okay because it probably isn't, you fucking liar. SO GET TO IT.

Find That Special Someone (or not) ;)

Find someone in your life that you can actually talk to. I don't mean bullshit conversations, I mean really talk to. Even though I stated before that any problems you have should be solvable by just yourself, having someone to talk to will benefit your life. After all, humans are social creatures. If you have something you need to rant about or something that you are excited about, talking about it with someone will help you solidify that positive thought/goal and it also helps you relieve any stressful/angry thoughts. Stop being antisocial and introverted. Although, if you are truly happier as an introvert, there is nothing wrong with that. Just don't lie to yourself. If deep down you want to meet more people and be more social, DO THAT. You won't know how it will make you feel to be more social if you don't try it. Now I don't mean talking to every fucking person you come across because you don't want to waste your time. Most of your conversations and interactions are useless. But, being a more social person will open up so many more opportunities in your life. Think about it. How many times have you thought about saying something to someone and didn't. This could be anything. Asking someone out, complimenting someone, being flirtasious, telling a stupid joke, etc. Friendships don't just come to you without a little bit of effort. The same goes for romantic relationships.Throughout this guide keep reminding yourself that you only live one life. Keep telling yourself that the time you have in this world is limited and what you have and what you can do will all be in the past within a matter of time (technically everything you are doing right now is instantly becoming the past). When you are old and just about out of time on this Earth, the last thing you will have left is memories. That's literally it. Memories of your whole life. What did you accomplish? Who did you meet, talk to, and what relationships did you start? Who did you help and influence, what amazing things did you do as a human being? What did you build and create? Who did you take care of and help? If you haven't even started to accomplish anything great, then the time starts NOW. You are going to make changes for the better. You are going to meet new people, get out of bad relationships, become healthier, become happier, and stop living in a depressing cycle of problems. You may be a happy person. You may have your life figured out or maybe you are starting to figure your life out. No matter where you are in your life right now: Happy, sad, or in between, you can ALWAYS do more, become more, and accomplish more. This is how successful businesses, relationships, and people ARE MADE. They are made with a strong, powerful, hard-working mindset. Great things are created by great people with great ideas. BECOME A GREAT PERSON. Like I said before, most of you know what you need to do to become successful in life. You just can't bring yourself to do the shit you need to do. There is no little secret for becoming a billionaire, having a beautiful relationship, or just being a happy person. You need to create that yourself with strength, motivation, and getting to fucking work. I think many of you can agree that at some point in life you need to grind. You need to work your ass off. Don't think there is an easy way of becoming great and successful. The longer you look for a secret path to success, the longer it will actually take for you to start on the right path of achieving your goals. FIND THE RIGHT PEOPLE. For your friendships, businesses, ect. You need to talk to and spend your time with the right people. Drop the fucking losers. They will slow you down. If someone in your life is not adding anything to it and instead taking happiness and energy away from you, you need to break off that relationship. It's not easy. Most of the time nothing easy is worth doing. It's hard when your own family members or close friends are draining you. This is more difficult than cutting off relationships with just basic friends, but even then, you need to think about yourself and what will make you happier and more successful. Keep reminding yourself, "I got this one life and what do I need to do to make it great?" Relationships, friendships, and human interactions have a massive effect on your life and its direction. You know who you should and shouldn't be interacting with. If you are confused, then just think about what this person adds to your life. If they are taking things away from you like your energy, happiness, and attention, then think about if that relationship is worth keeping. If it isn't worth keeping, end it. If a change needs to be made, you need to make that change fucking now and not wait. It's like if you are going cliff jumping - if you do that sort of thing. You are standing there on that cliff and you are hesitating. If you are hesitating because you think the water is too shallow, then obviously you shouldn't be considering jumping. But in this particular situation, you saw people jumping before you and they were completely safe. Not only were they safe but they were happy, maybe even ecstatic. They may have been scared, nervous, and fearful (like you may be feeling right now about tackling a problem in your life), yet they went for it. That weight was lifted off their shoulders, and they felt so good after jumping. If you just stand there and are too fearful to jump, you need to JUST JUMP. Your friends might even be cheering you on, motivating you to go for it. Your own self is probably telling you to just fucking do it. But that fear, that shitty fear sitting in the back of your head is making you hesitate. You may know you are going to jump but you keep telling yourself you need a little more time. Let's say you spend the whole fucking day at this cliff jumping spot and then finally, after fucking hours, you jump. And it was GREAT. You felt amazing afterwards. Now you could have done that hours earlier, felt better sooner, and jumped even more. Apply that little analogy to any situation that you need to conquer in your life. Especially apply this to relationships that need to be cut off or relationships that need to be started. You may know you need to do it, you tell yourself you are going to do it, but you wait and wait and wait. Maybe you wait so long that even more problems arise. Maybe you finally do what needs to be done and you realize, "holy shit, If I just did that sooner then I would be so much happier." The sooner you figure out how to better yourself, fix your problems, and grow, the sooner you will actually become happy. Think about how long you have been waiting to make a real change in your life. Think about what you have been postponing, putting to the side, and lying to yourself about. You might actually be surprised. There might be a ton of things in your life that you have been putting off. All these things just morph together into this blob of a thought that lives in your brain. You will start working out, you will find your soulmate, you will eat healthier, you will become more productive, and you will become a successful human being. This cluster of dreams and goals don't do anything but sit there as you continue living the same life. It is so easy to think about your goals and then just keep going about your everyday routine. Here is another analogy. Let's say you are a teenager in highschool. You aren't doing too great in school and maybe you are just getting by with high enough grades to keep your parents happy. Maybe you are dumb. Maybe you have shit grades and don't care. Let's pretend you do care about your grades. Let's pretend that you want to start studying more, you want to start working harder, and pay attention more in class. You tell yourself all of this after you fail a test. You went into school knowing you did not prepare enough, knowing you could have focused harder in class, and you knew your dumbass was going to fail that fucking test. So the same day after you take that test, before you go to bed, you make a promise. You say to yourself, "I'm going to get my shit together. I am going to study, focus, work, and become a better fucking person". You fell asleep so fast that night because you were confident in making this change which made you happy and content. Your mind was locked onto this new goal. You were excited about this new person you were about to become. This new hard-working you, who will accomplish great things. So you wake up early as fuck in the morning. It's maybe Tuesday or Wednesday, another shitty school day. You go to school feeling exhausted because you had to wake up early as hell and you don't like school because it's boring. Guess what thought is not crossing your mind throughout that entire day. All the shit you told yourself the night before. ANOTHER ANALOGY THAT APPLIES TO

EVERYTHING IN YOUR LIFE. You tell yourself the things you want to hear and then keep living the same way. You motivate yourself and hype yourself up because it makes you happy and excited but you don't ACTUALLY CHANGE. THIS IS A LIE. You are indeed lying to yourself. So here is what you need to do. You can and should still hype yourself up and use motivating self-talk but go at it differently. You need to make small changes in your life in order to become that great person. It is exciting and easy to just say a bunch of motivating shit to yourself and then just rely on those words as if saying those things will magically make changes happen. The problem is that your new goals and aspirations are TOO MUCH. You need to start small. And this is exactly what I am going to be talking about in the next chapter baby. LET'S GO! Also, don't necessarily assume you will be fine cliff jumping just because someone else did it before you and was fine. Stay safe out there.

The Path of Little Changes

NEW YEARS. OH MAN I AM SO EXCITED. Not only am I SO excited for a fun new years party but holy guacamole, a new year!? I am going to accomplish so much, do great things, become a LEGEND. I am not only going to start waking up at 5:00AM everyday and go on a 45 minute run, I will also go to the gym like 5 times a week. Probably do a nice little bro-split and just get absolutely shredded. In addition to that, I will start a couple businesses. A dropshipping business, maybe a plumbing business, and oh yeah I want to go back to college and get my masters degree in philosophy. Look at you inspiring yourself, getting prepared to become an amazing success in this new upcoming year. Guess what dumbass, you didn't do any of that. For the first couple weeks of the new year, you woke up kind of early. But 5:00AM? Fuck no. You couldn't wake up that early if your life depended on it. And running every day for 45 minutes? Your joints started aching after running for 10 minutes on your first day of the New Year. Starting businesses? You work a full-time job as a waiter at the Brigantine, or Hooters, or wherever the fuck. You don't have time for that shit. Boom. All of those goals and aspirations slowly dwindle as you find yourself continuing the same sad life that you promised to change for the better. That was a slight exaggeration. The point is: stop setting unrealistic goals. And stop trying to do a bunch of shit at the same time. Start small. If you want to start waking up earlier, you need to go to bed earlier and maybe start waking up at a time a little more reasonable than 5:00AM. If you want to start running more, start with a shorter run only a few

149

times a week. If you want to get fit and healthy, choose a work out plan and diet plan that fits you. It's okay to start small and work your way slowly and carefully to success. The same goes for starting a business. Slow down there buddy. If you work full-time, is it reasonable to think that you will be able to start a business and do all of those other things you were talking about? Probably not. Start small, reasonably, and carefully. Put time and effort into researching the best ways to achieve the specific goals you want. For you people who are already successful and phenomenal, it may be easier for you to really get to work and get shit done. You may be able to achieve multiple goals at the same time, but remember, practice makes perfect. If you know you aren't a "go getter", start slower and simpler when trying to achieve greatness. Create that powerful mentality by achieving your goals one by one and doing things the right way.

ALSO, you don't need a big event in your life to make you feel like you should change. That's so lame. Don't wait for a new year or a new this or that in order to actually start making fucking changes. Like seriously? That is like the whole cliff jumping analogy I talked about earlier. You are just waiting and waiting because you are fearful and even though you keep telling yourself that you can achieve this goal, you feel like you need more time. I know you have heard those success stories of people who had a very difficult life, who had to struggle and suffer through horrible circumstances. The same people who went through all of these difficult experiences have become extremely successful. Horrible situations or events in someone's life may contribute to the desire to work harder and become victorious. You DON'T need something like this to change for the better or start working harder. You can inspire yourself to become triumphant in life. Although, even though people have the power to motivate themselves, they still wait for stupid events like New Years in order to start working harder. You will use these catalysts as excuses in order to continue living the same life because you are comfortable where you are. Create a plan, write shit down, and do research. This is all vital when trying to achieve something in your life. And as I said before, do not make unrealistic goals, it will get you nowhere. You are just feeding yourself these lines in order to stay content and happy. So get to it my friend. Jeff Bezos, Elon Musk, and Serena Williams are all people. Guess what dummy? You are a person too. Any successful person had a goal and they achieved it. They didn't feed themselves unrealistic goals. Or maybe they did at one point but it didn't work out. So what did they do? They changed their mindset. They did their research, they worked hard, worked smart, and created a strong mentality by following through with what they told themselves they could accomplish. Athletic legends, billionaires, and celebrities. They all had goals and thoughts about achieving success just like you, so why are they so successful and you might not be? That's because you are doing it wrong. Apply effort and smarts to every situation, especially when you are going to start performing the steps it takes to accomplish your dreams. It is pretty crazy actually. We tend to put extremely successful people on pedestals. They were all once babies who could only say goo goo gah gah. Isn't that fucking funny. At one point the richest man in the world, the best athlete, the strongest bodybuilder, the most out-standing actor, and even the most powerful person on Earth was once a helpless little human who relied on others to survive. JUST LIKE YOU. Yes, they may have been raised in a different environment and were provided with different opportunities compared to you. But that doesn't matter because you have the internet. You can learn anything and everything on the internet. For starters, Youtube has literally every guide for everything that you have ever wondered about. Starting a business, investing, and pretty much any super important skill. The best part is you can find high quality videos of people explaining step by step how to do something. AND IT IS ALL FREE. I guarantee that you could learn the same amount of information if not more information about a certain skill with YouTube versus a literal college class. The entire internet can provide you with plenty of knowledge for any subject you are interested in. Don't be shy, search away. You can get fucking degrees and licenses now through the internet. You can take college online for fucks sake. But honestly you don't even need to go through college with all of the information on the web. School is seen as important mainly because you want good grades. In highschool, you wanted As. To get good grades you had to learn the information. Do you think you actually felt motivated to learn the information you were being taught or do you think students are motivated to learn through the desire to get As and Bs? This changes in college considering you are at a point where you are specifically learning about a career (more or less). But still, it will always be seen as school. You need to change your mindset about learning and education. Stop looking at it as a chore. Look at it as an opportunity to learn something that can make you more money.

You Can Be Anything

Get up and look in the mirror. Look into your eyes and really understand where you are in your life. Let your natural emotions flood into yourself. What are you feeling? What thoughts are lingering about. What feelings are washing over you? You may be anxious, depressed, happy, ecstatic, motivated, excited, high as fuck, or maybe you are a combination of a bunch of emotions. Remember you are yourself. Don't let this world, your environment, and all the bullshit in life separate you from yourself. Don't let your brain create thoughts that make you unhappy. This is kind of hard to explain and I am having trouble understanding this entirely. All you need to do is re-read this book a few times and you will be set. Also remember to love yourself, get some help if you need it, and become that person you want to be. You can be anything. Stop lying to yourself. Stop living in the same shitty cycle. Become who you want to be. Just remember to start the right way and do a little bit of research before you begin your life-changing journey. Unrealistic goals and self-talk that that doesn't get you anywhere is STUPID. Like I said before, the crazy goals that you can't accomplish all at once or the aspirations that are way too difficult for you to accomplish are hindering you from growing properly. Obviously, you should have an ambitious mindset. I am not saying to stop thinking like a beast but when it comes to ACTUALLY DOING SOMETHING, instead of just fucking telling yourself shit, you need to create a realistic and achievable objective. Back up your self-talk with real actions and changes. Self-talk is a huge part of becoming successful. Even though I explained before that some self-talk can be dangerous and hinder you, the right type of self-talk combined with the right type of work ethic can create enormous amounts of success. Let's say you finally are getting to it. You created a realistic goal. Maybe you want to actually start a drop-shipping business or something. You know it is going to take a lot of work and time but you start slowly and you do plenty of research. You literally did research on HOW TO research. You are starting where you should be, at ground zero. Let's say you have a full time job. So every night you set a timer for like an hour and spend that time researching how to create this new business. You shut your fucking phone off because you wil be distracted if you don't and you tell everyone you live with to leave you alone for just this one hour because you need it to research. Let's say you are consistent with this method. Months go by. HOLY SHIT. You have enough information to start your own business. And guess what? Because you started the right way by doing proper research, eliminating distractions, and you focused on your goal, you actually made it very far. PAUSE. Before I continue this amazing analogy, we need to take a dive into TIME. Time is always going by. If you want to actually do something productive for a certain amount of time, do not let yourself be distracted. If you give yourself an hour to research, fucking research. You need to give it your all when you do anything productive. The same goes for working out and other important shit. PUT IN MAXIMUM EFFORT every time you are doing something that matters.OKAY. Back to this little story about you creating this dropshipping business. You are proud that you not only created an achievable goal but you were also actually productive during the times you needed to be. So you start your business. You have to spend some money to get started. But you know how to spend it and you know what to do. You realize you know exactly how to start making money with this business, what products to sell, and what to do if something goes wrong. A handful of months go by. You are making real money. Woah, this is actually going a lot better than expected. Years go by. You invested the money you made with that dropshipping business into reliable stocks that you did plenty of research on and now you are close to a million dollars in your portfolio. Congratulations, YOU DID SOMETHING. Now create that objective and fucking go for it. Use motivating self talk every time you are about to do something important. Hype yourself up, tell yourself that you fucking got this. Get to where you want to be. ACHIEVE THAT GOAL. Motivate yourself throughout every part of the day. Tell yourself you are amazing, you are a winner, you will conquer every fucking challenge and obstacle that gets in your way. Once you know how to start something correctly and how to begin achieving that task, you will have an infinite drive and you will never want to quit. Your self talk needs to be backed up with an evident drive for endless success. Now some of you might be thinking that this information is too vague. I keep saying, "Once you know where to start". You may be thinking, well how do I know where to start? Everyone is different. Everyone wants something different. Even if you want to do the same thing as someone else like get fit, start a business, ect. You may have the same goal as someone else, but don't be mistaken, everyone is very different. Although, everyone can start achieving their goals the same way: LOOK UP HOW TO DO IT. Don't just read and invest yourself in the first damn thing that pops up on Google. Figure out what information is useless by reading reviews and getting input from others. I am here to guide you on what you need to create a better life and how you need to go about doing it. Creating a better life can mean a number of things. Usually it starts with making yourself happier, more successful, and healthier. Choose something. I would start with being healthier and see where that takes you. Once you get that down, create another objective. Maybe you want to make more money. What do you need to do to make more money? Do you want to learn a new skill, create a business, or start investing? Maybe all of the above. CHOOSE SOMETHING. AND STICK TO IT. Give yourself a certain amount of time every day or every other day to achieve this goal. And remember: PUT IN MAXIMUM EFFORT.

Things You Should Do Everyday

Now you know how to start your journey. Whatever the fuck it is. Here are some things you should do every single day in order to feel great and not get mentallly exhausted. Drink water. Actually start drinking more water. I know you have heard that before. Drinking enough water will increase your energy, promote weight loss, flush out toxins in your body, as well as improve your skin. Half a gallon is probably enough, although, if you are active and you work out, a gallon a day might be necessary. But DON'T overdo it. If you drink too much water, you will literally piss out all of the important minerals in your body like sodium, magnesium, and potassium (electrolytes). Your pee should be light yellow (if your pee is clear, you are literally dehydrating yourself from drinking too much water). Find the right dietary supplements. Humans nowadays lack a lot of nutrients that their body needs to function at full capacity. I recommend checking out Ancestral Supplements. This company has some of the best dietary supplements on the market. From beef organs to bone marrow, they pretty much have everything. If you need something for stress and anxiety, I recommend looking into Ashwagandha. This ancient medicinal herb is absolutely amazing and you should start taking it ASAP. Not only does Ashwagandha balance your cortisol levels (this reduces stress/anxiety), it also fights depression while even boosting fertility and testosterone. This is just a start. Depending on what your goals are, physically and mentally, there is a massive list of supplements that can help you become healthier and happier. Just don't over do it and also don't waste your money on shit that doesn't work. Start stretching, rolling out your muscles, and maybe even getting into yoga. Stretching and yoga is important even if you don't lift weights or exercise normally. Stretching can decrease back pain, prevent injury, and improve your range of motion. Yoga can help you manage stress, benefit heart health, as well as improve your flexibility. Some form of stretching is important and should be added to your daily or weekly routine. If you exercise normally, rolling out your muscles can be great for decreasing tissue tension and improving your range of movement. Meditating is pretty effective but you should only take time to meditate when you have everything else in check. Obviously a healthy diet and a good exercise routine is important. SLEEP. Okay, this is fucking huge. You need to sleep, and you need to sleep well. Now if you have any sort of problem, I guarantee insufficient sleep is related to that issue. Chronic sleep deprivation can cause obesity, high blood pressure, depression, heart failure, and a lot more. Now you may not be chronically sleep deprived but even moderate or light sleep deprivation can cause so many complications. What causes a lack of quality sleep? It could be a variety of things. A lot of times people blame stress and anxiety for a lack of sleep. So figure out what makes you anxious, and fix it.

Also make sure you fix your breathing. A lot of people have enlarged tonsils, oversized adenoids, a deviated septum, or even swollen turbinates. All of this can affect how much oxygen you get while you sleep which directly affects the quality of your sleep. Over a super long time, humans have developed shitty facial bone structures. The major issue with these bad bone structures is that it negatively affects how we breathe. This unfortunate bone structure development occurred due to a change in our diet and lifestyle. Hundreds of thousands of years ago, humans used to hunt animals, carve them up, and eat them on the spot. They would eat everything, including bone marrow. At one point, they weren't even cooking the food. They would chew and chew and chew. This chewing created super strong jaws and bones. This vastly different diet and way of living allowed humans to develop strong mouths, open airways, and a prospering facial bone structure. When food started getting cooked, our brains expanded causing our airways to become slightly smaller. Although, this wasn't a major problem. Then, processed food came along and fucked everyone over. Softer, esiar to eat food completely ruins the ability for the bone structures in our face to develop properly. Anyways, If you have any sort of congestion problems or breathing issues, TALK TO YOUR DOCTOR. Seriously, figuring that shit out will change your life. Now, what are your physical goals? Understand your physical goals before you start researching what workouts you should do and what you should be eating. Some people want to get super big, some people want to get super shredded, and some people just want to be healthy and not overdo it. Although, no matter what your goals are, keto and intermittent fasting have some phenomenal health benefits. So I recommend at least trying that out to some extent. Be more social, make more eye contact, and if you do find yourself in a conversation, do your best to make it meaningful. Start doing things that make you focus and make you work hard. When you choose to devote time to a task, give it your all. Really try and stick to one task at a time. Put your damn phone in a drawer if you have to. If you set aside an hour to get some work done, how much of that time is spent checking our phone? If you actually devote an hour of time to get something done and you ELIMINATE all distractions, you will be amazed with how much you can actually achieve in such a short amount of time. Stop giving up. Use positive self talk every single morning and throughout your whole day. Eliminate the unrealistic goals that I talked about earlier. Take what you learned from this guide and apply it to every part of your life. If you don't do that, then I have failed you. The material in these pages was meant to spark something in your soul. My goal is to inspire you, motivate you, light a flame under your inner strength and tenacity. I honestly wanted you to get a little bit angry when you read this. Anger creates energy and persistence, and that is what you NEED in order to become successful. You need to be fucking persistant and be determined to complete every task you are faced with. Good luck my friend. You fucking got this.

Last Edited: February 28th

It is currently October 28th. It has been exactly 8 months since I have touched this book or guide or whatever the fuck this is. Why is that? Because I am a human and, just like you, I sometimes can't finish things I put my mind to. That's fucking ironic. This guide is essentially supposed to permanently put an end to your procrastination and all the other bullshit that keeps you from becoming the most successful person you can be, and the person writing it doesn't even practice what they preach. BUT, I don't care. Listen. You are going to fail and fail and fail and fail and……… yeah, fail. You are going to put your mind to something, stick with it for however long and then BOOM, before you know it you have spent the last 3 months watching netflix and doing fuck all in your free time instead of chasing your dreams and getting shit done. Our brain releases dopamine (the primary drive for every decision) for things that are easy to do and bring us immediate happiness. Our brain craves the quickest way to achieve a dopamine release. Think about what makes you extremely excited or happy. Having sex with a hot person, thinking about eating something very delicious (probably unhealthy), achieving something in a video game, watching a movie, ect. Now think about how excited you are to sit your ass down at a desk and spend the next 2-3 hours learning about how to start a business. Ice cream or 2-3 hours of trying to learn something new. Hmmm. An excessive amount of sugar and fats that are easily accessible (and prehistorically essential to our body's functioning and survival) or something that doesn't bring any immediate happiness? Yup, your thoughts, feelings, and your own fucking brain will do everything it can to get what it wants. That FUCKING ICE CREAM. The dopamine release connected to that ice cream outweighs learning about how to start a business by 1000%. This goes for any task in your life that is actually difficult, challenging, and takes up time. It does not bring instant satisfaction. It is very hard to overpower that dopamine craving for things that give you instant satisfaction. Going out with friends versus staying in to learn. Your thoughts will try to convince you to go out with your friends because it releases that dopamine. Thousands of years ago, dopamine was what kept humans alive but now it is keeping us from living our best life. You definitely need a dopamine detox. I don't really care to explain it so just google it. To be honest, you could read a bunch of guides like these, watch a ton of videos about how to be successful, but the real secret is just to stop being a fucking pussy. Like seriously. You probably work your ass off, maybe you don't, but if you really want something like passive income, financial freedom, physical and economic success, you need to spend a lot of time and work figuring out where to start, how to start, and actually fucking starting. For example, let's say you want to create some sort of business. You need to begin at level fucking 0. You won't see any results, especially not financial results, for a very long time. You need to be able to break past that barrier again and again in order to keep growing your knowledge and learning more and more about what you need to do in order to become successful. Let's go with a more conservative amount of time you might need to spend on trying to create a business. Let's just say 1-2 hours a day. Seems easy right? I mean if you work 8 hours a day, what is 1 to 2 hours learning about something that will bring you so much happiness in the future? WRONG. For example, you might spend a night after work doing research and putting in the time but then what about the next day and the day after that. I guarantee that you are going to lose that initial drive you felt almost instantly. That's just how it is. Your dopamine sensors are all fucked up and the last thing you want to do after work is what your brain thinks is more work. But what if you could change the way you think about "working"? What if you could change your brain? Instead of looking at this task as being some boring work that you need to get out of the way in order to get your ice cream. What if you felt excited about learning new things and coming up with ideas for a business? What if you were more excited about that than eating ice cream or playing video games? Then you would be unstoppable. If you woke up in the morning and instantly had a drive to spend hours and hours of that day to learn and acquire new knowledge, you would be successful before you fucking know it. This is possible. It is possible to change how your brain perceives "work" and "tasks''. Unfortunately, it isn't easy. But I promise you, if you start setting aside time everyday to work on something that will bring you closer to your goal, you will start seeing results. And no, I don't mean financial results (that comes after some time), I mean the effect this will have on your brain. It's just like growing a different muscle in your body. It takes time, consistency, effort, and persistence. The most important thing to keep in mind when you are working towards your goal is to put 100% effort into whatever you are doing and completely remove all distractions. But start small. It is going to be a challenge at first. If you are consistent then you will slowly start to see results. When you start to see results, whether it be income or just making connections and new ideas (as well as strengthening your discipline), you will start to build a healthier relationship with what once was a task that you wanted to get out of the way.

You Are Not Your Thoughts

Ronald works 9-5 at a fucking paper factory and his life kind of sucks. Sure he goes out with his friends sometimes, has a relatively good-looking girlfriend, and makes just enough money to stay afloat and enjoy himself once and a while. RONALD WANTS MORE. Ronald has been wanting more for a while. What do I mean by "wanting more"? Well, think about what you want to gain from reading this guide. You want to make more money, be more successful, become financially free, and WIN AT LIFE. So back to my little example. Ronald has been wanting to start an online business for months. When he is sitting at his desk, wasting away, he has these moments of intense motivation and inspiration for starting his own business. He will think of all the possible success, income, and how much reputation he will gain by creating an amazing business. He will daydream multiple times throughout his work day, and in some cases, he will be extremely eager to get home so he can begin the process of creating a start-up. It's Tuesday (work was awful, boring, mindless, and depressing) and Ronald is going to clock out in an hour and head home. He cannot wait to get home, grab a snack, and start researching business ideas. He is about halfway home, stuck at a stop-light five minutes away from his house. He forgot that he told his girlfriend he was going to call her on his way home. So he calls her and they chat it up. He gets to his apartment, gets out of the car, and heads up to his room. HIs girlfriend says, "Hey baby, let's get some food and watch this new show on Netflix" (Ronald's girlfriend doesn't live with him). Ronald thinks to himself, "hell yes, I want food, I want to see my girlfriend, and I want to watch this new show". BUT, right when Ronald is about to get ready to go to his girlfriend's place, he remembers about this whole business venture he wants to take on. He thinks to himself, "Ohhhh, well, you know what, I worked my ass off today and I deserve to chill and see my girlfriend". BOOM. All that motivation, excitement, and eagerness for starting a business he had during his work day - POOF - GONE - NADA. So, Ronald goes and hangs out with his girlfriend and they watch the first couple episodes of Squid Game. At 11:30, he heads home. "Oh man I was really going to get started on that business research", "Well I'll have plenty of time tomorrow". Tomorrow comes and he decides to go drinking with his buddies after work. Before he knows it, weeks go by without him properly sitting down and consistently trying to take the steps necessary to starting a new business. Okay, back to reality. Sorry about how cliche, basic, and lame that example was. Anyways, what I am trying to get at here is that it is extremely easy to feel motivated and inspired to do something in the moment. It releases dopamine which our brain is constantly striving for. But actually putting effort into something that our mind perceives as "boring" or as a "task" is very difficult to do. So that's why Ronald and hundreds of millions of other people are going through this constant cycle. You have gone through or are currently going through this cycle. You have aspirations that get you through the day but when it comes down to it, when you have free time to actually put in the effort to obtain your dreams, you go off and do what will give you the quickest dopamine release. STOP DOING THIS SHIT. You aren't making good results because you aren't actually putting in the time and effort. Your mind might be completely occupied with thoughts that are about creating a business. But actually getting to work and starting is what 99% of people struggle to do consistently. Your brain, thoughts, and feelings all want dopamine NOW. Your thoughts relate to feelings. This is pretty obvious but I'm going somewhere with this, trust me. Let's go back to Ronald. He is THINKING about this business venture all day which creates FEELINGS of inspiration and essentially happiness which triggers a dopamine release from the BRAIN. But then, when he calls his girlfriend, his thoughts are somewhere else completely. Because he likes his girlfriend, his thoughts have now transitioned to things relating to and revolving around his girlfriend. These thoughts, like eating with his girlfriend, having sex with her, and watching a show with her produce excited and happy feelings which trigger dopamine. Stick with me here. Now, this dopamine, triggered from the stimulus of talking to his girlfriend (and her asking him to come over and whatnot) completely outweighs the dopamine triggered from the excitement of researching business ideas when he gets home. WHY? Because all of the shit he can do with his girlfriend is easily accessible and brings him instant happiness. Your brain knows this from previous experiences. Because your brain is literally an organ in your body trying to keep you alive, and because dopamine is linked to things that basically keep you alive, your brain now wants "hanging out with your girlfriend" more than "doing business research." So, this is why Ronald is rationalizing with himself on why he should go hang out with his girlfriend. Even though he knows that researching business ideas is what HE wants, his own fucking brain literally creates thoughts that make him want to do something else so his body can get this fucking dopamine. Okay, here is the takeaway. When you want to do something that will bring you great success in the future, like building a business, you need reasons in order to start the actual work. These reasons could be financial freedom, building something, or fulfilling your purpose. Unfortunately these reasons, which your brain knows can only be achieved after years and years of hard work and consistency, don't produce as much happiness (or dopamine) compared to things like hanging out with friends, drinking, eating out, playing video games, ect. This is why your own brain will constantly try to rationalize eating something you shouldn't or any of the number of things I mentioned above. THIS IS ALL YOU HAVE TO DO. If you can identify with a purpose that YOU ACTUALLY BELIEVE brings you more happiness than all of these other little moments of "quick happiness", you will ALWAYS, WITHOUT FAIL, be able to put the more important things first (sorry for that long sentence). Like researching on how to start up an online business or whatever it is that you have been putting off for months.

Dealing With Fear

I'm going to keep this chapter short and sweet. So you know that fear is the mind's mechanism of keeping you alive. Back in the good old days, fear is what got you away from that giant fucking bear chasing you up a tree. Nowadays we are afraid of talking in front of an audience. How pathetic is that. We are afraid of making sounds with our mouth in front of other people. Like who fucking cares? You are just talking. But for some weird reason, all on its own, your mind releases these chemicals. These chemicals that make you feel anxious, worried, or fearful. Now there are things that we know literally don't matter at all and we still get scared of them, like social anxiety. Things that pose no danger or threat whatsoever still make us afraid. I like to look at this as a misfire. Your brain, historically, has used chemicals to make you anxious in situations that pose a threat to your existence. And talking in front of people isn't a threat to your life, but your brain sure as hell thinks it is. Why? It's probably due to how advanced our species has become. Your prehistoric brain function has not yet adapted, therefore, the wrong chemicals will be produced for the wrong situations. If you can simply look at fear as your friend, and by that I mean look at it as a chemical (which it basically is) that is just trying to keep you alive. Perceiving fear this way allows you to deal with situations in a different light. With this new understanding of fear, you can step back and truly analyze: Why am I feeling this way? If you can confront the actual threat (95% of the time there is no real threat) then this anxiety and fear will dissipate. Now what if you are making a business decision? What if money is involved? Now this creates a lot of fear within an individual. Especially when you are sinking money into a new business venture or something of the sort.

www.ingramcontent.com/pod-product-compliance
Lightning Source LLC
Chambersburg PA
CBHW060332030426
42336CB00011B/1306